"Dignity is something we all possess but may not readily understand or recognize as being part of our true nature. *Awakening Dignity* offers teachings and practices that help us see and deal with any obstacles in our way. Written with clarity and a pertinent connection to our daily lives, you don't need to be a Buddhist to gain insight from this lovely book."
—Sharon Salzberg, author of *Lovingkindness* and *Real Change*

"Phakchok Rinpoche is an emerging stakeholder of the Buddhadharma who has trained under some of the greatest teachers of the century. His efforts to create a dialogue between the Buddhadharma and Western philosophy and thinking are greatly welcomed."
—Dzongsar Jamyang Khyentse Rinpoche, author of *The Guru Drinks Bourbon?* and *Living Is Dying*

"In this delightfully engaging book, renowned teacher Phakchok Rinpoche teams up with scholar and longtime student of Rinpoche Sophie Wu to offer us an entirely accessible yet truly profound exploration of dignity as stable confidence in our own true nature. Awakening and cultivating our innate dignity cures us of feelings of low self-esteem, inadequacy, self-doubt, and incompleteness. With 'dignity training' exercises—contemplative practices that help us to touch and grow our innate dignity—along with edifying stories and lively examples, this is a jewel of a text, and genuine medicine for what ails us."
—Jan Willis, PhD, author of *Dreaming Me: Black, Baptist, and Buddhist* and *Dharma Matters: Women, Race, and Tantra*

"The concept of dignity is one that many of us think we understand, yet precious few truly do. Personally, I was among them until reading this book by Phakchok Rinpoche. Although I have long worked on cultivating compassion and wisdom, it was only after reading *Awakening Dignity* that I realized the essential role dignity plays in understanding who I really am and my full potential. Rinpoche's heartfelt gift to the world is to provide the knowledge and path for learning that dignity is our pure nature beyond how we usually identify ourselves. To begin on the journey to realizing our inner dignity, we need an introduction, and this book is it."

—Kit DesLauriers, 2019 US Ski and Snowboard Hall of Fame, two-time World Freeskiing Women's Champion, and author of *Higher Love: Climbing and Skiing the Seven Summits*

"In this book, Kyabgön Phakchok Rinpoche taps into the essence of fearless dignity and provides a step-by-step experiential process to gently clear away the layers of 'clouds' (habitual patterns) that obscure certainty in our innate basic goodness. In this way, Rinpoche guides us to recognize our own true nature and deftly illustrates how such recognition is an essential first step in seeing the fundamental nature in all beings. By providing the tools for stabilizing this clear view of unchanging reality, Rinpoche helps us cultivate the skillful means to treat ourselves and others with more awareness, loving-kindness, compassion, and wisdom. I wholeheartedly recommend this book for all who wish to find happiness and fulfillment in their lives."

—Yongey Mingyur Rinpoche, *The New York Times* best-selling author of *The Joy of Living*

Awakening
DIGNITY

A Guide to Living a Life of Deep Fulfillment

PHAKCHOK RINPOCHE
SOPHIE WU

SHAMBHALA

Shambhala Publications, Inc.
2129 13th Street
Boulder, Colorado 80302
www.shambhala.com

Cover art: David Stubbs Photography + Motion
Interior design: Katrina Noble

9 8 7 6 5 4 3 2 1

First Edition
Printed in the United States of America

Shambhala Publications makes every effort to print on acid-free,
recycled paper.

Shambhala Publications is distributed worldwide by Penguin Random
House, Inc., and its subsidiaries.

LIBRARY OF CONGRESS CATALOGING-IN-PUBLICATION DATA
Names: Rinpoche, Phakchok, 1981–   author. | Wu, Sophie (Shu-chin),
    author.
Title: Awakening dignity: a guide to living a life of deep fulfillment /
    Phakchok Rinpoche, Sophie Wu.
Description: Boulder: Shambhala, 2022.
Identifiers: LCCN 2022011535 | ISBN 9781645470885 (trade paperback)
Subjects: LCSH: Buddhism—Doctrines. | Dignity—Religious aspects—
    Buddhism. | Religious life—Buddhism.
Classification: LCC BQ7795 .R56 2022 | DDC 294.3/42--dc23/eng/20220404
LC record available at https://lccn.loc.gov/2022011535

CONTENTS

Foreword by Daniel Goleman and Tara Bennett-Goleman vii

Introduction 1

Part One: Your Nature Is Pure

1. The Mirror of the Heart 9
2. Know Yourself 24
3. Beyond the Beautiful and the Ugly 43
4. Three Meditation Teachers 56

Part Two: You Can Change

5. Making Friends with "Sticky Mind" 67
6. Noticing, Not Judging 86
7. Healing from the Habit of Judgment 97
8. The Courage to Love 106
9. "Who Am I?" 125
10. The Compassion to Act 142

Part Three: Gaining Certainty and Trust

11. Authentic Power 165
12. Dignified Living and Dying 184
13. Carefree Ease 201
14. Continuing the Journey Home 211

Dignity Training Exercises 224
Notes 225
About the Authors 230

FOREWORD

When we arrived for a week as guests of Nyoshul Khen Rinpoche and his wife, Damchola, at their home in Bhutan, our hosts shared their extreme delight with their last guest, who had also been studying with Rinpoche and left just before we arrived.

His name: Phakchok Rinpoche.

From childhood on, Phakchok Rinpoche had received teachings from great Tibetan Buddhist masters, starting with his grandfather Tulku Urgyen Rinpoche—one of the most revered Dzogchen meditation masters to have left Tibet for Nepal when his country was invaded. Nyoshul Khen Rinpoche, too, was counted among that revered group of great spiritual masters, for both his inner realization and his scholarly expertise.

Phakchok Rinpoche took the teachings of both Nyoshul Khen Rinpoche and Tulku Urgyen Rinpoche to heart, practicing them in his daily life, in compassionate action, in retreat, and in his own teachings and studies. His studies were mainly in a traditional *shedra,* an intensive course of textual immersion that takes years to complete. Rinpoche emerged with the Tibetan equivalent of a PhD.

Even more significant, through his years spent in retreat, Phakchok Rinpoche has achieved more than intellectual understanding of the teachings—he has come to embody them. Like others in his illustrious family of Rinpoches, his very being radiates wisdom, compassion, and dignity.

We've known Phakchok Rinpoche since he was young—meeting him when we traveled to Nepal to study with his grandfather Tulku Urgyen Rinpoche—and always found him wise beyond his years. Today he has become a remarkable teacher to the world, offering the traditional wisdom teachings in a fresh and unique way that makes them accessible to everyone—not just those who practice in the Tibetan tradition.

In this book Phakchok Rinpoche, with the able help of his student and adept writing partner Sophie Wu, shares his profound insights into "dignity," a stable confidence in our true nature. Even as we are transforming the shortcomings that come up in our lives, he explains, we can turn toward our own true nature, like seeing the clear sky behind the clouds.

Early in the Covid-19 pandemic when much of the world went into lockdown, Phakchok Rinpoche moved into a holy cave in Nepal for an extensive retreat. We were touched that he asked an assistant to contact us to make sure we were okay. His warm, caring heart, together with that wisdom beyond his years, make Phakchok Rinpoche an inspiring teacher for these times.

Phakchok Rinpoche is a living example of what he teaches, modeling for us all his natural wisdom. His confident dignity shines, even when he acknowledges his own challenges and shows how he brings awareness to the inner work of transformation. This openness, mixed with his refreshing candor and humor, makes what he teaches all the more relatable to our own lives.

Rinpoche has an unusual sensitivity when it comes to his Western students (perhaps aided by his wise-hearted wife, Norbu, who grew up in an eminent traditional Tibetan family in the Washington, DC, suburbs). He has repeatedly been remarkably proficient at communicating teachings to his students according to their needs.

Awakening Dignity offers us all a powerful, clear, and friendly guide, a path to our own true nature, through teachings and practices that help us see what obscures our pure awareness.

DANIEL GOLEMAN AND TARA BENNETT-GOLEMAN

Awakening
DIGNITY

INTRODUCTION

On an autumn day in Kathmandu, near the famous Boudhanath stupa, a few friends and I were enjoying Nepali masala omelets and steaming hot chai for breakfast. At one point, the conversation turned to how deeply healing and positively life changing Phakchok Rinpoche's teachings on dignity had been for us and many of our friends. I suggested producing a brisk work, compiling a few of Rinpoche's talks on the topic into a small book. "It should be quick and easy," I said. Or so I thought. That initial idea was the genesis for what would, eventually, become the current book. I proposed the idea to Rinpoche. Rinpoche liked it, and I began to work. That was 2016.

Quickly, the project took on a life of its own, expanding far beyond the original conception to its present form. I came to realize that Rinpoche's teachings on dignity are not limited to the relatively few talks in which he made it the principal topic. In fact, the notion of dignity is present, whether explicitly or implicitly, throughout the wide array of Rinpoche's teachings. Therefore, rather than merely compiling a few talks as I had originally intended, I found myself combing through a much larger body of Rinpoche's teachings extending over a fifteen-year period. Expanding the source material in this way enabled me to place the topic of dignity within the broader context of Rinpoche's overall teachings.

I also sought to situate the topic of dignity within its historical meanings and common usage. Dignity is not a new idea—it is a perennial topic in western culture, fascinating philosophers and informing political and ethical discussions for millennia. Even so, the exact meaning of dignity has remained unclear. For many months, I researched and read about dignity across a broad spectrum of thinkers, including Buddhist masters, Western philosophers, theologians, lawyers, psychologists, and social activists. I then discussed my findings with Rinpoche. Even though most of this research does not appear explicitly in this book, Rinpoche permitted me to use these perspectives and ideas to contextualize his teachings within a broadened framework comprehensible to contemporary, global audiences.

Rinpoche and I met several times over the course of five years in different parts of the United States and Asia, and on Zoom, to discuss the book, brainstorm ideas, formulate presentation strategies, and later, to finalize the manuscript. Over the same five-year period, Rinpoche gave more extensive teachings on dignity in Singapore, Nepal, Japan, the United Kingdom, Austria, Germany, and various parts of the United States—teachings which proved invaluable to the project.

Phakchok Rinpoche was born in 1981 in Kathmandu, Nepal, to a family of famous Tibetan Buddhist masters, including his father, grandfather, and uncles. At the age of one, he was recognized as the seventh Phakchok Rinpoche, the reincarnation of the previous Phakchok Rinpoche and holder of the Taklung Kagyu lineage in the Tibetan Buddhist tradition. He was enthroned at age six. Rinpoche has studied under many accomplished spiritual masters, principal among them Tulku Urgyen Rinpoche (his grandfather) and Nyoshul Khen Rinpoche. At age twenty-two, after extensive and formal training in all aspects of Tibetan philosophy and practice, Rinpoche was awarded the title *Khenpo* (comparable to a PhD in Buddhist philosophy) from the Dzongsar Institute of Advanced Buddhist Studies in Bir, India. Afterward, Rinpoche began actively traveling the world teaching Buddhist philosophy, theory, and practice.

Straddling two worlds, Rinpoche grew up in a traditional Tibetan Buddhist family and culture while (unlike Tibetan teachers of previous generations) also enjoying ample contact with people from all over the world. He is extremely interested in getting to know the difficulties, concerns, and struggles facing people of contemporary global culture. Wherever Rinpoche has taught around the world, he has asked students: "What are your questions?" "What are your struggles?" What followed were ubiquitous stories about low self-esteem, self-hatred, self-doubt, body harming, addiction, and fear of aging and dying. Rinpoche's teachings on dignity are a response to these concerns.

Drawing from the Tibetan Buddhist wisdom tradition, Rinpoche teaches dignity as an inherent quality of fundamental wholeness and completeness that all people possess. This understanding is often rendered by Rinpoche with the phrase "our nature is pure." This book aims to show that everyone already possesses dignity as a natural inner quality; we merely need to learn how to access and recover it by transforming our emotional and neurotic patterns. Rather than feeling helpless and passive in the face of difficult situations, aligning with our inherent dignity provides a sense of power and agency. Dignity is power, and we are inherently powerful.

During our early meetings, Rinpoche said the book should be written with straightforward language and made accessible to secular readers as well as seasoned Buddhist practitioners. He instructed me to draw from various angles and approaches to present the topic in a full, systematic way. In line with Rinpoche's intention, the book is organized into three parts that reflect both the development of dignity as a concept and the progression by which dignity is cultivated. The first part of the book introduces us to the mind and its genuine nature—that which we must come to know as fundamentally pure and rich. The second part focuses on understanding the habits and confusion that obstruct this pure nature and the methods for dealing with them. The third part concentrates on the result of this process—a profound and deeply rooted trust and confidence that reflects a transformation in our relationship with ourselves, others, and the world.

As Rinpoche stresses time and again, an intellectual understanding of dignity is of limited value—real transformation only comes from direct experience. "Experience, experience, experience," he emphasizes. Accordingly, as an adjunct to conceptual understanding, this book offers a set of contemplative and meditative exercises—collectively called dignity training—designed to help readers connect with and cultivate their own inner dignity. Virtually all chapters conclude with one or more dignity training exercises. Readers are encouraged to work with these practices as they read through the book, and to continue working with them long afterward, according to their own inclination and motivation.

Most of us tend to seek "band-aid solutions" to life's problems, looking for the easiest, most expedient response. Rinpoche has a compassionate understanding that sometimes this approach is necessary. Still, when it comes to our relationship to ourselves and the world, thinking in this way will not create lasting change. In this book, Rinpoche painstakingly guides us to dive deeper in examining the source of our confusion. He repeatedly reminds us to check ourselves, both when things are going well and when things are not going well. Rinpoche underscores that self-knowledge gained through direct experience is the key to stabilizing our dignity and living a meaningful life.

This encouragement for us to check ourselves is not an instance of "do as I say, not as I do." Nor are we left without a clue as to what the path to dignity might look like. One of Rinpoche's unique qualities is that he frequently teaches from personal experience, openly sharing his own struggles and how he has worked to overcome them. By joining and commiserating with our experience, Rinpoche shows us precisely—through example, as well by word and deed—how we too can free ourselves from our own confusion. The example of Rinpoche's own learning process validates our experience and bolsters confidence in our own capabilities. On this account, this book includes several of Rinpoche's personal stories as well as illustrative stories of his students and friends, most of whose identities have been altered for the protection of privacy.

Many people behind the scenes have supported the fulfillment of this project in myriad ways. I extend my heartfelt thanks to all of them. Joshua Fouse, Ani Tsunma Jamyang Donma, Hilary Herdman, and Vera Leung provided audio recordings and written transcripts of many of Rinpoche's teachings. Stefan Mang checked all Tibetan and Sanskrit terms and provided helpful research. Tsepak Rigzin offered additional advice on the use of Sanskrit and Tibetan terms. Margaret DeWind kindly made herself available for proofreading and copyediting throughout the process. Mary Sutphin, Marjorie Rhine, Andrea Sherman, and Kevin Gormley read the entire manuscript and offered helpful feedback and suggestions. Many other generous friends, too many to name, read and provided helpful comments on the proposal or portions of the book.

I am very grateful for Casey Kemp, our editor at Shambhala Publications, who shepherded the process in such a calm and skillful way. Her expertise, kindness, care, and clarity in communication made the publication process easy and pleasant. I am thankful to Natasha Kimmet for her expert and precise copyediting and to Peter Schumacher and Gretchen Gordon for helping to bring this project to completion in its late stages.

Most special thanks go to Alan Pope, my husband, whose roles in and contributions to this book are too numerous to count. Foremost among them were carefully editing the entire manuscript, offering many constructive suggestions, and encouraging and supporting me every step of the way, including those days when I could only scrawl a few lines. Without him, this long process would have been much more arduous and less joyful and fulfilling.

Finally, I cannot adequately express my appreciation to Rinpoche himself for kindly entrusting me with this important project.

Spending years soaking up the heart advice of an authentic Buddhist master while collaboratively making that advice available to a wider audience is an unspeakable honor and privilege. I am deeply grateful. I also want to thank Khandro Norbu Gyari for her valuable advice and indispensable role in providing all the support I needed for this project while bestowing upon me her extraordinary warmth.

Those who have met Rinpoche know that words cannot convey his lively presence and interpersonal style of teaching. Even with many present, Rinpoche directly engages everyone in his audience, generating the feeling that the teaching is for them personally. The kindness and confidence in his eyes, the non-judgmental warmth he naturally radiates, the spontaneous and playful gestures—all these communicate so much more than can be translated into words. Nevertheless, I did my best to convey the essence of Rinpoche's teachings, and I apologize for any shortcomings on my part. It goes without saying that I am responsible for any errors or mistakes in this work.

In the Western tradition, Socrates said, "Know thyself"; in this book, Rinpoche helps us do just that. The teachings here are not mere rhetoric, nor are they religious belief. They are living wisdom complete with the methods necessary to contact, affirm, and cultivate our own inner dignity. I only wish these teachings had been available to me at an earlier stage in my life, but I am happy they are available to you now. The current host of serious problems facing the world today—the global coronavirus pandemic, climate crisis, extremism in all its forms, and more—make it especially urgent that we look deeply into our own experience and reevaluate what is truly important in life. It is my sincere hope that this book will provide support for that process and benefit you, your loved ones, and the world.

SOPHIE (SHU-CHIN) WU

Part
One

———

Your Nature Is Pure

Mind is the cause for the arising of wisdom;
Don't search for buddha elsewhere!

THE BUDDHA[1]

1

The Mirror of the Heart

It is only with the heart that one can see rightly;
what is essential is invisible to the eye.

ANTOINE DE SAINT EXUPÉRY[1]

One day, while sitting on the porch of my retreat center in Cooperstown, New York, a student asked me, "Rinpoche, I have so many faults. How can I ever have dignity?" This young man had been coming to our annual summer meditation retreat for years. He is physically robust and mentally sharp, owns a thriving business, and recently married his soul mate. By conventional standards, he is regarded as very successful in life. Nevertheless, on this occasion, he asked me this question with a sense of desperation. Despite his success in love and work, he feels little confidence in his basic personal worth.

"I am working all the time, and I don't feel that I deserve a break. No matter how much I work, I feel that I am not enough—in my work life, in my personal life, in my self-care, in my friendships. I am not enough in my efforts to help the world. I am not enough in anything I do. And I feel that I must perform perfectly all the time in order to be loved," he lamented. I found myself thinking, "*Nyingje*, poor guy." *Nying* means "heart" in Tibetan, and *je* means "king." *Nyingje*, king of the heart, is the Tibetan word for compassion. I often say this word silently to myself when I encounter a suffering being. It is a way of relating to their pain and wishing for it to go away.

This student's words of dissatisfaction and self-doubt were especially striking. Only a few days earlier, he had charged into my living room breathless, elated to tell me about the expansion of his business. Now, he looked like he was faltering on the brink of a cliff. His joy had evaporated without a trace, his self-confidence in ruins. Yet such dramatic fluctuation in joy and confidence is not peculiar to this student—it is extremely common. I know this from my own experience, and I think almost everyone else knows it, too.

Why is the joy inside us so hard to maintain? Why are we so easily lured by self-doubt, inadequacy, fear? Why do we feel so incomplete? What is the cause of this kind of suffering and what, if anything, can we do about it?

You Are Not Alone

Frankly, this student's life experience could not be more different from my own. He grew up in New York, the largest and most cosmopolitan city in the United States, whereas I was raised in a Buddhist family in Nepal, a small country in South Asia. He received public education and developed his own private business, while I underwent formal monastic training to teach Buddhist meditation. Yet despite these different backgrounds, his question reminded me of my own fears and vulnerabilities, my own doubts and hesitations, and in particular, my own youthful confusion about dignity. I know how he feels!

It is very common these days to speak of "low self-esteem," meaning that we have a low opinion of ourselves. So many people experience these feelings of not being enough—of not measuring up to what is expected of us—that we assume this is normal. Feeling this way is like standing on a shaky foundation, powerless and unsure about who we are and what we are doing here; everything seems to be falling apart. The discomfort we feel is usually a faint murmur, but sometimes it erupts into an extremely unpleasant storm. This is the experience of lacking dignity and questioning whether it is something we can ever have.

By contrast, certainty in our dignity makes us unshakable in the face of any circumstance. We have a deep understanding of who we genuinely are, with an unwavering sense of purpose. But such dignity is something we must achieve.

In some ways, my own confusion about dignity has been especially unsettling. People address me as "Rinpoche," a Tibetan word commonly translated as "precious one." It is typically used as a term of respect and reverence in addressing someone recognized as the reincarnation of a revered teacher. While still an infant, I was recognized as a reincarnate lama, or *tulku*, from one of the lineages of Tibetan Buddhism. In my mother tongue of Tibetan, *la* means "life force," and *ma* means "mother." A reincarnate lama is revered in my culture as a mother-like figure who in previous lifetimes demonstrated remarkable spiritual achievements, and who in this lifetime is supposed to embody many good qualities, such as dignity, compassion, and wisdom. Hence, a reincarnate lama is supposed to nurture and guide other people. But when I was young, I was shy and self-conscious and easily felt uncomfortable in social settings. When approached by strangers who came to visit me or my family, I often was overwhelmed by uneasiness and would rather hide than have any contact with them. How would it be possible to nurture and guide other people while struggling with my own shyness and insecurity?

And yet I have since become a teacher, traveling the world.

In the past fifteen years, during my teaching tours throughout the Americas, Europe, and Asia, the question of how to develop dignity has come up again and again. Many of the people I have met, regardless of differences in age, gender, and background, have shared with me how they were plagued by a lack of dignity and expressed their desire to obtain it. In doing so, they told me many stories. One person fell out with her friend, felt betrayed, and bemoaned the shattering of trust between them. Another was wounded by his broken family and persistent domestic violence. Another expressed anger toward his ex-wife, whom he perceived to have interfered in his relationship with his son. Even though some events had happened years or even decades earlier, many people continued to be haunted by lingering feelings of pain, grief, fear, sadness, and anger. On the surface, they might have appeared to others to be fine, but inside they were struggling. Even though the stories that triggered their bitter experiences were different, the expressions of disappointment in themselves were similar: they chided themselves for "losing their dignity" when dealing with difficult situations or emotions.

"I hate myself."

"I am such an idiot."

"I do not deserve to be loved."

"How could I have done (or said) that?"

These were some of the common expressions of having lost dignity. But when I asked them what exactly they had lost—that is, what they meant by dignity—they offered only vague and ambiguous answers. They told me, for instance, that dignity means "respect," "self-esteem," "self-worth," or "courage."

An American philosopher named Ruth Macklin argues that "dignity is a useless concept. It means no more than respect for persons or their autonomy."[2] But Martin Luther King Jr.'s reverence for this concept was made clear when he told a group of students at Barratt Junior High School in Philadelphia, "Number one in your life's blueprint should be a deep belief in your own dignity."[3] These are powerful and inspiring words. For Dr. King, dignity was not a vague idea that could be reduced to "respect" or "self-esteem." Nor was it something abstract and ephemeral. He used the word *dignity* to denote an important quality related to who we are and what we do in our lives. Maybe it is hard to define dignity because it points to something in us that we don't yet know well enough to describe. To define dignity clearly, we may need to understand ourselves more fully.

The Western Faces of Dignity

Before we go into how to understand ourselves more fully—the predominant focus of this book—we might briefly consider how dignity has been regarded in Western culture. *Dignity* derives from the Latin word *dignitas,* which means "worthiness." Therefore, the earliest question regarding dignity was "Who is worthy, and of what?" The society of ancient Greece in effect gave the following answer: "People of high social status are worthy, worthy of respect." In other words, when seen through the lens of social hierarchy, the notion of "worthiness" is easily reduced to the respect that others pay you. Of course, personal worth is not intrinsically linked to social hierarchy, and indeed, over time the meaning of dignity has evolved to encompass the recognition that all human beings have worth. But the notion of equating this worthiness (or dignity) with respect continues to this day.

Many religious and philosophical thinkers had other ideas, envisioning dignity as something larger than respect. For example, in medieval times, the important Catholic thinker St. Thomas Aquinas regarded dignity as an intrinsic value that is part of God's creation. The Italian Renaissance scholar named Giovanni Pico della Mirandola, in his famous work *Oration on the Dignity of Man* (1486), equated dignity with God; he reasoned that because we are made in God's image, we become worthy, or dignified, by raising ourselves up toward God. The eighteenth-century philosopher

Immanuel Kant gave a secular interpretation of dignity as an inner quality that is "an end in itself" with unconditional, incomparable value. Kant regarded dignity as a fundamental moral principle, famously declaring that people should always be treated as ends in themselves, never as means to be used for other ends.

Kant's famous motto has inspired a connection between the two historical understandings of dignity. How? Regarding human beings as ends and not means affirms our inner dignity while also demanding that this inner dignity be respected through social and political justice. Today, activists for human rights and social justice frequently invoke a statement in the United Nations' Universal Declaration of Human Rights (1948), which begins: "All human beings are born free and equal in dignity and rights." That is, we all have inner dignity. This document later asserts that "recognition of the inherent dignity . . . of all members of the human family is the foundation of freedom, justice and peace in the world."[4] That is, this intrinsic dignity must be respected.

This is just a sampling of the different ways dignity has been taken up in Western culture. There are still many debates about what dignity really means, but they generally revolve around the two notions just described: dignity is either something within us that is reflected in our actions, or it is something outside us that must be granted by others.

Guardian of Our Most Precious Qualities

From the Buddhist perspective, these two senses of dignity are intimately interrelated. For example, our own intrinsic dignity compels us to treat others with dignity; at the same time, treating others with dignity is a way of affirming and expressing our own intrinsic dignity. As you can see, the Buddhist understanding emphasizes inner dignity, seeing it as foundational to all expressions of dignity.

There is no magic bullet to solve the myriad world problems facing us today. The Buddha's teachings, though originating more than 2,600 years ago, are based on our actual human condition. We know when we fly on an airplane that if an emergency occurs, we must first put on our oxygen mask before helping other people with theirs. Similarly, a guiding principle of our human condition is that to bring change to the world, we must first change ourselves. In the Buddhist understanding of cultivating dignity, this means that we must first know our mind, which is the basis for all experience. Only when we understand our mind can we know what we offer the world. To heal the world, we must first heal ourselves.

What is this mind that we must first come to know? In the Buddhist tradition, mind and heart are often used interchangeably. For example, the Sanskrit word *citta* translates as both "mind" and "heart." The heart used here does not refer to the physical organ. And mind is not our ordinary state of consciousness (*sem* in Tibetan), but the mind's pure nature (*rigpa* in Tibetan). Because this heart-mind signifies the union of compassion and wisdom, it is sometimes referred to as the "noble heart."

According to the Buddha's teachings, everyone is endowed with a noble heart. *Everyone*, without exception. Our noble heart is the source of infinite potential and profound qualities, even though they seldom fully manifest. Still, it makes a tremendous difference in our experience simply to know with confidence that we are intrinsically endowed with the precious qualities of this noble heart, which include kindness, love, compassion, wisdom, and dignity.

In Tibetan Buddhism, the tradition in which I grew up, we describe the experience of dignity using several Tibetan terms. The one that conveys the meaning of dignity used in this book is *lha-yi ngagyal*. *Lha* translates into English as "innate nature." *Ngagyal* is "pride" or "confidence." Therefore, this type of dignity means "pride or confidence in our innate nature." Or we could say "unwavering trust in our noble heart." This is very different from understanding dignity as a human right, an ethical principle, or simply respect. The sense of dignity I am using here relates to our essence and our nature. It is at the very heart of our being.

This same Tibetan word (*lha-yi ngagyal*) sometimes also translates as "vajra pride." The Sanskrit word *vajra* refers to the diamond—the sovereign of all stones. A diamond is so strong and solid it cannot be crushed. Unlike vajra pride, ordinary pride can easily be crushed. It is associated with negative emotion based on an inflated ego. When the ego is inflated, it can be easily punctured, like a balloon. This vulnerability leads us to devote a great deal of energy to protecting and cherishing the ego, a role that ordinary pride serves. Vajra pride, by contrast, is deeply rooted in our inherent pure nature. When we have vajra pride, we have nothing to prove, and we trust ourselves completely. We don't make comparisons, nor do we succumb to feelings of superiority or inferiority. Vajra pride points to a foundational and unwavering inner strength and power devoid of the various wants, needs, and insecurities of ego pride. This is the reason why vajra pride is sometimes also known as "divine pride" or "stable pride."

When I speak of dignity in this book, I refer to the power that comes from knowing decisively that our heart is noble, our nature is inherently pure. We are whole and complete. It is the opposite of feeling that we are not enough. Dignity is not a passing state; it is an unwavering trust. This unwavering trust in ourselves acts as our protection against life's ups and downs. It enables us to see situations clearly and respond appropriately. In dignity, we are not riddled with uncertainty and self-doubt. Rather, we can notice our own mistakes and correct them. It is a way of seeing, and it is a way of being.

Part of the power of dignity, or vajra pride, is that it serves as the guardian of our most precious qualities. Whereas ordinary pride attempts to guard our fragile, inflated ego, dignity protects our most precious inherent qualities, such as loving-kindness, compassion, and wisdom. With dignity, we perceive things as they actually are, and we perceive ourselves as we actually are. This clarity of vision and understanding protects us from the distraction and confusion that ordinarily lead us to question ourselves and our reality. The result is a profound and powerful sense of inner stability. Like a diamond.

We Are Inherently Wealthy

As human beings, it is unavoidable that we make mistakes. Mistakes occur over the span of an hour, a day, a year, a lifetime. In the absence of vajra pride, we tend to experience these mistakes with an extremely personal sense of failure. If mistakes are unavoidable, why do we beat ourselves up so badly that we only see negativity and forget about our most precious qualities? Instead of feeling bad "for" ourselves, we feel bad "about" ourselves. We are sometimes the worst roadblock to our own dignity.

Tibetan Buddhism uses a traditional metaphor to illustrate this type of confusion. We are like an impoverished person living in a tiny shack. We feel that we have nothing of value and must venture outside in the world to seek riches and wealth. We don't realize that buried underneath our shack is a vast treasure. The treasure is right here, within our reach. We need only find a way to access it.

This image shows how oblivious we are to our fundamental nature. Seeing ourselves as poor, inadequate, and incomplete creates impediments to knowing ourselves and the richness of our qualities. This impoverished mentality leaves us constantly wanting, never having. We feel deficient, as though we can never do enough, let alone be enough. We treat ourselves severely, without the same kindness we might extend to a complete stranger. This mentality is rooted in the mistaken way we see ourselves.

Two Mirrors

A student who is a psychologist told me of a concept called the "mirror stage" of human development. By the age of six to eighteen months, infants or toddlers develop the ability to look at a mirror and connect the image they see with themselves. The first time this happens, they are exuberantly happy. The only problem is that while the image in the mirror is indeed their reflection, they mistakenly think that this reflection is them. In identifying with this image, they eventually identify with an idea of who they are. Later in life, others "mirror" back to them what they see: "you are good," "you are bad," "you are pretty," "you are ugly," "you are smart," "you are stupid." Their subjective judgments further shape their self-image, influencing how they come to see themselves and their world. When they compare this self-image with the idealized images of society, it always falls short. No wonder we lose all trust and faith in ourselves. No wonder we search outside ourselves for validation from other people. No wonder we always feel like we're not enough. We are mistaken about who we really are.

The Buddhist tradition speaks of a different mirror—a different way of seeing ourselves. This is the mirror of the heart-mind, which we could abbreviate as either "mirror of the mind" or "mirror of the heart." What is reflected by the mirror of the mind? It is the light of wisdom, our innate knowing endowed with the energies and qualities of clarity and wholesome purity. In other words, this mirror reflects what is intrinsic to us. It shows us who we really are, beyond our usual ways of thinking about ourselves and others' distorted perceptions of us. In the mirror of the mind, we see and know ourselves in a direct and complete way. The first mirror reflects the ego; the mirror of the mind reflects our actual self.

We all can experience and know this actual self, which the Buddhist tradition calls "buddha-nature." The word *buddha* means "awakened one." It signifies someone who is fully awake or fully liberated from mistaken notions of who or what they are. This has nothing whatsoever to do with being "Buddhist"—this potential is within all of us. When we can always recognize and maintain our true nature with complete trust and certainty, the quality of unshakable dignity is naturally present, alongside love, compassion, and wisdom.

Returning Home

Given that so many of us wrestle with feelings of incompleteness, inadequacy, and spiritual homelessness, how can we ever contact and actualize our inherent dignity? Or, as the student asked, "How can I ever have dignity when I feel so bad about myself?" This book is a humble answer to these questions. It is a road map for returning home to our natural state of being.

When we are out of town, many of us use a GPS to guide us home. But a GPS can only point us in the right direction. We must travel the road to get there ourselves. It is the same for the journey home to your own true nature. Therefore, in this book I will not focus on theory or philosophy. Instead, I will provide practical instructions for you to travel the road to your own inherent dignity.

In 2004, I visited New York City for the first time. On a bustling city street, I felt so free. Nobody knew, or cared, who I was. I loved the freedom of anonymity! Looking back, however, I realize it was not just the anonymity of a big city that forged my sense of freedom; it was in large part because I no longer felt crippled by the shyness or self-consciousness of my youth. My heart had learned to be more open and connected. I felt at home. The journey from imprisonment by my own emotions to the freedom of my inner experience was guided by many kind teachers in the Tibetan Buddhist tradition. It has become a source of self-knowledge, and the result is more valuable than all the material wealth of the world.

As I will illustrate in the next chapter, countless great meditation masters have used these methods to fully realize dignity in themselves. What I share in this book springs from the heart advice and meditation training I received from my teachers, who themselves received these teachings from an earlier generation of teachers, in an unbroken lineage that traces all the way back to the Buddha. But what these teachers taught about dignity applies to everyone, not just Buddhists. Although this book is based on Buddhist teachings, it is not intended to be a Buddhist book. Nor is it intended to be a religious book. It is written with the intention to benefit anyone who aspires to live a dignified life and wishes to help others.

Taking the Journey

How can we take this journey to our genuine home, our noble heart? This book offers "dignity training" designed to achieve this very goal. Dignity training consists of a set of contemplative and meditative exercises included at the end of almost every chapter in the book. Using these tools to train regularly and repeatedly will lead you to the firsthand, direct experience of dignity rather than a mere conceptual or intellectual understanding.

To cultivate dignity, we must first train the mind. At present, our mind is wild, pulled in this direction or that based on how we habitually respond to what we see, hear, or think. But we may not even realize this at first. Nowadays, we are very familiar with our smartphones, but we are not so familiar with our own minds. Dignity training provides the tools we need to start knowing our minds and seeing how they operate. As a result, our minds will become calm and peaceful, pliable and workable, so that we can see ourselves very clearly.

This process can be unsettling at first. We are nervous about what we might find if we look deeply at who we are. But dignity training is not about trying to get rid of things we don't like about ourselves. It is about learning to accept ourselves fully. When we gain familiarity with our habitual reactive patterns and how they trap us, we also come to realize that we are not these patterns. Consequently, we begin to recognize new and healthier possibilities for responding to life situations, including whatever had previously triggered negative emotions in us. When this happens, we have begun the journey to recognizing and realizing our inherent dignity.

Before we learn how to apply these tools for the cultivation of dignity, I want to make a distinction between training and practice, two terms that are often used in a variety of ways. In this book, "training" refers to the formal process of working with our minds through contemplation and meditation. "Practice" is applying what we have learned through formal training to our everyday lives. This book provides you with the tools you need to conduct the formal training, but it is up to you to apply it in your life and to verify whether you are making progress.

Let me put it simply:

Formally working with your mind is training; applying the training in everything you do is practice.

We train formally with whatever time we have available, but then we practice in the context of our everyday activities. The "effort" of practice is one of relaxing the mind and noticing what we are doing. It is about choosing more consciously between beneficial actions and harmful ones. It is about releasing burdens, not taking them on. At first it may seem challenging, but eventually it becomes something we wouldn't want to live without.

We can begin dignity training where we are, right here, right now. To have a healthy body, we build our muscles through physical exercise. To have a healthy mind, we build the "muscles" of our mind through meditation training. But it is important to remember that in dignity training, the process takes place in our heart. Now is the time we stop looking down on ourselves and instead cultivate complete trust in who we really are!

<hr />

DIGNITY TRAINING

Your Relationship with Inner Dignity

Sit quietly, alone. Relax your mind by breathing naturally and gently for a few minutes. As you mentally ask yourself the following questions, do not seek answers, but let the answers come to you.

> How would you describe dignity in your own words? What does this concept mean to you? (Do not search for the term on the internet.)
> Where does your understanding of dignity come from? For example, is it based on what others have told you, what your heart tells you, or some other source?
> What is your own relationship to dignity as an inner quality? Can you relate to it? When do you have it? When do you not have it? Think about specific instances in your life.
> Start noticing your relationship to dignity throughout the course of your day. Occasionally check in by asking yourself, "What is the state of my mind? Where is my dignity?"
> Be honest with yourself, without judgment.

Being without judgment is the key. This exercise is for you alone. There is no one to please and no one to validate or invalidate you. Be very gentle toward whatever emotions arise and know that you need only be honest and sincere. There are no right or wrong answers. In fact, you may want to return to these exercises throughout the course of your dignity training—if you do, almost certainly your experiences and perceptions will have changed.

With this first exercise, we are discovering our working basis for cultivating dignity. In this process, we must begin where we are, knowing that we can change. And, ironically, we can only change when we completely accept where we are. Therefore, be loving and accepting toward yourself and what you find—that, in itself, is a display of your inner dignity.

Inspirational Support

> Whenever I tell a story, I always avoid the two short-comings of exaggeration and denigration—neither adding any extra qualities that someone does not possess nor refusing to acknowledge the qualities that are truly present.
>
> TULKU URGYEN RINPOCHE[5]

Know Yourself

There is nothing on earth that is not medicine.
TIBETAN SAYING

A famous Tibetan story about medicine goes as follows. One day, an herbal doctor asked his apprentice to find a natural substance that has no healing properties. The apprentice thought to himself, "This will be easy. I'll be back in no time." After years of searching and searching in the Himalayas, he returned to his master empty-handed. The apprentice could not find a single substance on earth without healing properties. Even poison, he learned, can be transformed into medicine to be used for healing.

The Great Physician

Buddhist texts often metaphorically refer to the Buddha as a doctor and his teachings as medicine. In this sense, the Buddha was a healer. But any effective doctor must have a clear diagnosis of the patient's condition and provide an appropriate remedy accordingly. The life story of the Buddha shows how a young prince named Siddhartha discovered ("diagnosed") the ultimate condition to be cured and the remedy for overcoming it. Today, more than 2,600 years later, the same condition continues to afflict people, and the same remedy applies.

As a prince, Siddhartha could very well enjoy the title, power, and material wealth into which he had been born. But even inside the luxurious, sheltered palace where his father the king sought to protect him, Siddhartha felt an inner discomfort. He did not understand this discomfort until, on four occasions, he managed to escape the palace walls to see what was on the outside.

The first time Siddhartha left the palace, he encountered an old man. "What is that?" he asked. "Will I become like that?" "Yes, everyone becomes old," replied his attendant. Siddhartha's father, wanting to protect his son from all signs of suffering, had permitted him to be approached by only the young and beautiful. Siddhartha's first encounter with a visibly old person made him realize that everyone who is born will become old.

On the second occasion, Siddhartha saw a man who was sick. "What is that?" he asked again. Having a human body, being sick is inevitable, he learned.

On the third occasion, Siddhartha saw a corpse being carried away for cremation. "What is that? Will I die?" he asked again. Siddhartha realized that even if one is a king or a prince, once born, he will eventually die.

Illness, old age, and death are part of our basic human condition. They are inconvenient truths that no one can avoid. And yet many, like Siddhartha's father the king, are determined to deny them.

When Siddhartha left the palace for a fourth time, he saw a wandering holy man. Unlike the expressions of sadness, pain, and dissatisfaction that marked the first three individuals, this man's face looked remarkably content and peaceful. Strongly impressed, Siddhartha recognized that it might be possible to find freedom from the suffering of the human condition. "How does one achieve freedom like that?" he asked himself.

Siddhartha intuitively knew that answering this question required leaving the comfort and security of his royal life. At the age of twenty-nine, he left the palace to search for a way to cure the illness of human suffering and attain liberation from it forever.

Siddhartha studied with different meditation teachers and quickly mastered what they taught. Although he achieved highly refined states of meditative concentration, he still had not realized complete liberation from suffering. So Siddhartha next practiced with a group of ascetics. Starving himself, he sometimes consumed only one grain of rice and one drop of water per day. He slept in charnel grounds, lay on beds of thorns, burned in the sun, and endured cold at night. But his suffering did not end.

Recognizing that neither extreme exertion nor extreme physical punishment were providing the freedom he sought, Siddhartha tried a different approach. He sat under a Bodhi tree in Bodhgaya, in northeast India, and meditated with tremendous resolve. After a few days and nights, early one morning Siddhartha attained the realization of emptiness. This means that everything that we perceive with our physical senses and our mind is without a separate, independent existence. In other words, it has no intrinsic existence. Everything is interdependent with everything else. Abiding unwaveringly in the true nature of mind, Siddhartha was completely free from all hopes and fears, suffused instead with the qualities of love, compassion, wisdom, and dignity. He had achieved enlightenment. Siddhartha had become the Buddha.

Recall that the word *buddha* means "awakened one." Siddhartha did not earn the title "Buddha" because of his high social status, wealth, or political power. He earned it because he listened to the inner stirrings of his dissatisfaction—the same dissatisfaction that you and I know—and he embarked on a path to overcome it. Using the physician metaphor, he didn't strive merely to treat his symptoms—rather, he delved deeply into his own mental experience to identify their causes and overcome them. That is why he is also known as "The Victorious One," signifying his victory over any forces obstructing him (and us) from being free, happy, and peaceful.

The Buddha spent the next forty-five years of his life teaching what he had learned about the causes of suffering and how to overcome them. By following his teachings, his disciples in turn achieved their own liberation, only to pass the same inspiration on to their students, and so on. This lineage of student-teacher transmission has continued unbroken to the present day.

As I grew up in a Buddhist family and community, the story of how Siddhartha became the Buddha had a powerful and inspiring effect on me. Rather than conforming to the commonly accepted value of worldly success, Siddhartha radically questioned its validity. He discovered through meditation and direct experience that the mind holds the key to our happiness and suffering. If we pursue working with our mind, we eventually find that we already possess everything we need to be free, happy, and peaceful. Our nature is already enlightened. Before we realize this, however, we are caught in confusion and negative emotion. Because our nature is pure, we can purify these mental poisons and transform them into medicine. We start with recognizing that the secret to enlightenment is inside us, not outside us. We start with confidence in our inner dignity.

The Buddha's insight and wisdom are still potent medicines today, centuries after the Buddha's passing. Nothing prevents us from applying the methods he taught for purifying our mental poisons and transforming them into wisdom. But the Buddha taught us never to blindly believe in his teachings or those of any religious system. For this reason, he emphasized that we should carefully examine his teachings and determine for ourselves whether they are true. He diagnosed our illness and prescribed the medicine. But it is up to us to take the medicine and verify its effectiveness.

The Great Magicians

My journey from an insecure boy in Nepal lacking inner confidence to an outgoing world traveler with many international friends was not a straight line. Throughout this process, I was accompanied by the inspiration of numerous spiritual masters of the past and present whose own life stories demonstrate that transformation is possible.

A student who loves Tibetan literature once said to me, "Tibetan literature is so vast. What should I read?" I told him, "Read *namtar*." A namtar is the life story of an accomplished spiritual master. The Tibetan word namtar is commonly translated as "complete liberation." A namtar is not a story of worldly success. Instead, it demonstrates how a spiritual master has questioned commonly held values, embarked on a road less traveled, and achieved liberation by following in the footsteps of the Buddha. Captivating as it is, a namtar does more than entertain us or satisfy our curiosity; it inspires us to emulate the spiritual masters and achieve what they have achieved.

I love reading namtar, especially the stories of the *mahasiddhas*, who bear similarity to the saints in the Christian tradition. Considered the founders of a meditation tradition called Mahamudra, the mahasiddhas are people who, by virtue of practicing meditation, achieved what are known as *siddhis*. Siddhis include both the attainment of wisdom and the attainment of miraculous powers. That is why the mahasiddhas are also sometimes referred to as the "great magicians." The mahasiddha literature tells the life stories of eighty-four such great magicians. Intriguingly, they came from all walks of life. Among them were a thief, a beggar, a philosopher, a gambler, a hermit, a housewife, a prince, and a peasant. You name it!

One of the most famous mahasiddhas is Milarepa, who as a young man murdered several people. Deep remorse and longing for spiritual practice led him to become a highly accomplished practitioner and important teacher. Another was a sesame oil maker, a rich merchant. He lived a luxurious and indulgent lifestyle; for example, for each meal his servants prepared a lavish feast comprising eighty-four main dishes, twelve kinds of sweets, and five kinds of beverages. But then he met a teacher who pointed out that while selling sesame oil might bring wealth, it won't bring liberation. The sesame oil maker requested meditation instruction, practiced for nine years, and achieved enlightenment.

We might think that enlightened beings would all act the same way, but these masters were very different from one another. They had unique personalities and circumstances, and they confronted different challenges in life. But there was at least one thing they had in common. They did not accept anything at face value just because it was a popular belief or had been handed down for many generations. And they did not accept anything merely on the authority of others, including their own spiritual teachers. Instead they all looked inward, thoroughly reflecting on and investigating themselves and the phenomenal world. In this way, they connected with the qualities they already possessed, and they realized that their core nature is unshakable.

Some people have the romantic notion that the only path to liberation is as a yogi living in a cave, with knees made sore from meditating cross-legged constantly. On the contrary, the *mahasiddhas* of these stories were mostly householders with families and jobs, like most of us. They came from many different parts of India and Tibet, lived at different times, and received different types of meditation training. Their realization did not spring from a particular culture or a particular line of work.

These stories show us something that philosophy alone cannot. Seeing how ordinary people in ordinary circumstances have gained accomplishment and realization provides us a sense of possibility for ourselves. They become role models for our own journey of transformation and liberation. For Buddhists, other role models include the Buddha or Guanyin ("the bodhisattva of compassion"). For Christians, a role model might be Jesus Christ, Mother Teresa, or one of the Catholic saints. For civil rights activists, it might be Martin Luther King Jr., Mahatma Gandhi, or Nelson Mandela. Recalling the qualities of our role models can inspire us to emulate their example.

But in emulating their example, it would not help to try to look like them, speak their language, or follow their profession. You might become rich as a sesame oil maker, but that will not make you the mahasiddha sesame oil maker! The point is not to emulate them externally but to learn about what they cultivated internally, and then emulate that.

A Living Example

If the legendary stories of past masters provide such powerful inspiration, how much more inspiring and instructive are the living examples of contemporary teachers who embody the same qualities? They teach us not only by way of example but through their very words and actions. Because they are right here, their effect on us is more direct and tangible. My grandfather is such a living example to me, especially in what he taught me about dignity.

I still vividly remember the last time I visited my grandfather.

It was before Losar, the Tibetan New Year, in Nagi Gompa, a mountain hermitage above the Kathmandu Valley. My grandfather resided there for thirty-three years and taught meditation to numerous students coming from near and far. Because he was living with a deteriorating heart, my grandfather's body was very frail. My father wanted to bring him to the city of Kathmandu to be treated, but my grandfather preferred to stay at Nagi Gompa. During this final visit, my grandfather acted gently and calmly, in his usual way, without a trace of concern for his weakening body.

Not until later did I realize he had been arranging his worldly affairs and preparing others for his passing.

Upon my departure, my grandfather asked, "Do you really have to go?"

"Yes, I do, grandfather. I have classes to attend in Kathmandu," I answered.

At the young age of fifteen, I did not detect the hint that this might be the last time we would be together. Not long afterward, while people in Kathmandu were preparing for a big puja (a traditional ritual prayer ceremony) in celebration of Tibetan New Year, my grandfather passed away, peacefully, in sitting meditation posture. The way he died was no different from the way he lived: humble, stable, peaceful, calm, carefree, with kindness and compassion, and without fear. The way he lived and the way he died exemplified extraordinary human and spiritual qualities. He epitomized what I later realized was dignity.

Although my grandfather was the first to teach me dignity, he did not teach it as a theory or philosophy. Instead, he taught dignity first and foremost through his presence. Words seem inadequate to describe the qualities he exuded. No matter where I was, I could feel the wisdom, compassion, and warmth radiating from his small rooftop room at Nagi Gompa to encompass the whole world. I was deeply affected by this experience and aspired to be like him.

My grandfather, Tulku Urgyen Rinpoche, was a simple and humble person. He did not have big titles, never wore nice clothes, and was always content with little. He was one of the few meditation masters exiled in Nepal who had been fully trained in Tibet. Even though he was recognized as an accomplished meditation master, he never spoke about himself, let alone any of his accomplishments. Some may think that people who exemplify dignity must have strong presence, holding their heads high and standing like majestic rulers as portrayed in Hollywood movies.

But my grandfather was not like that at all. He was confident but not prideful. He was humble but not weak. He was compassionate toward others but not afflicted by their misery. And most extraordinarily, nothing could shake his core or hurt his feelings! This was not because he was numb or apathetic. Quite the contrary, it was because he was always aware not only of what was going on around him but also what was happening inside his own mind. When someone praised him, he remained firm and steady. When someone criticized him, he remained firm and steady. Nothing could shake him. When people pressured him into doing something with which he disagreed, he would not give in. He was like a small diamond, shining brightly and naturally, steady and strong, without any pretense and with total awareness and clarity. His dignity was stable and indestructible.

When we are steady and strong like that, we do not need outward validation.

I was seven or eight years old when my grandfather began to teach me meditation from the Tibetan Buddhist tradition. At that time, I was not mature enough to understand what I was doing. But growing up in an environment surrounded by Tibetan Buddhist practitioners, I have seen and heard about people who are not shaken by poverty, physical discomfort, illness, dying, or even other people's suffering. These include modest housewives and wealthy businessmen, people whom we do not commonly associate with spiritual accomplishment. I saw these qualities in my teachers, my father, my uncles, and in other genuine practitioners—in so many people who vary in character but display the same kind of solidity as that of my grandfather. They are like mountains, steady and unshakable.

My grandfather and many of my subsequent teachers taught me that regardless of gender, education, wealth, power, or societal status, our core nature is unshakable. Therefore, everyone has the same potential to develop enlightened qualities and to live and die with dignity. Being in the presence of living examples of dignity in my formative years was extremely encouraging and helped me aspire to live a dignified life. But what is the secret to becoming like them?

Many years after my grandfather's passing, when my inner experience and life experience had grown alongside each another, I learned that witnessing living examples is only the first step to developing dignity. We next must learn to experience dignity directly, and it is only then that we can truly develop it and undergo meaningful change.

Learning to Know Myself

As a young child, I was educated privately by my grandfather. Before his passing, my grandfather carefully arranged for me to continue my education at the Dzongsar Institute of Advanced Buddhist Studies in India, a respected institution of traditional Tibetan education for monks. That kind of educational training is called *shedra*. Discipline is strongly emphasized. Students study a large number of traditional Buddhist scriptures and often must memorize them. It usually takes nine or ten years to complete the education.

Shedra was a very different environment from what I was familiar with at home. I learned a lot. I studied all kinds of Buddhist texts. I was not as diligent as some of my classmates, but I could do well when I put in effort. I enjoyed making new friends. My teachers were very knowledgeable and kind. And I really loved philosophical debates, also known as monks' debates. In the hot sunny afternoons in India, with sweat dripping down our faces, a group of us would engage in debating different topics from our studies. It was fun! I remember one time when, after spending hours preparing for a debate, I defeated my opponents' points. I was so happy. My professor was so happy.

That happiness did not last. Only a few days later, my professor scolded me, and I didn't understand why. I took the scolding personally. Feelings of pride, self-consciousness, resentment, and hurt—combined with the anxiety and loneliness of being a teenager living away from home—surged in the form of anger. It was so difficult.

When I was a child, my shyness and self-consciousness were not a big deal and did not cause any problems. They were just part of my personality. But when I came to study in the shedra, my shyness and self-consciousness haunted me like a shadow. When I met new people, I had no confidence to talk to them. When I went to town, I always thought that people were looking at me and judging me. (I did look different in my monk's robes.) I was not free.

To compensate for my insecurity born of shyness and self-consciousness, I developed a habit of doing things to please people, secretly wishing they would love and accept me in return. When they were not pleased by me or what I did, I became confused, lost, and upset. The incident with my professor was such an example. I did not know how to make sense of being scolded after trying so hard to please him. My confusion turned into anger—not only with my professor and myself but with everything.

My Tibetan doctor diagnosed me as having too much "wind" (agitated mental activity) and advised me to return home to Nepal for two months of rest. If this were to have happened in today's Western culture, my diagnosis probably would have been depression.

A 180-Degree Turn

Not knowing what to do with my anger, I went to see Nyoshul Khen Rinpoche, my principal teacher after my grandfather passed away. He was in his sixties at the time, living in Bhutan.

Nyoshul Khen Rinpoche asked me, "What is the problem you are struggling with?"

"I am angry," I answered.

Nyoshul Khen Rinpoche continued, "What does anger look like?"

I was puzzled by his question. I widened my eyes and raised my voice to emphasize my earlier statement, "I am angry. And I am angry with *everything*."

"Yes, yes, I know." Rinpoche nodded his head with his usual gentle kindness.

"But what does anger look like?" he asked again. "Does it have shape? What is the color of your anger?"

My anger was so palpable. I could feel it when it welled up in my body. Sometimes I felt the anger so strongly that I wanted to shout. Yet I seemed unable to describe what it looked like, to know its shape or color. I had never thought of knowing my anger that way.

Nyoshul Khen Rinpoche then instructed me to focus on my breath, come back to the present moment, and look directly at my anger. To my surprise, the moment I looked directly at my anger and tried to find its color and shape, it slowly dissipated and lessened its grip on me.

I wanted, so badly, to tell Nyoshul Khen Rinpoche why I was angry. I was angry because my professor scolded me. I was angry because I did not deserve the scolding. I had one hundred reasons for being angry. I wanted to tell him my stories and my troubles. Nyoshul Khen Rinpoche just listened, quietly. He himself had lived for years with a long-term illness that had made his voice very weak yet never agitated him or deflated his spirits. He whispered to me, "Who is angry?"

"*I* am angry," I replied.

"Who is 'I'?" he pressed.

Nyoshul Khen Rinpoche's simply redirecting the question from why to who changed me, immensely. I began, though not immediately, to see that my anger was not caused by external conditions, as the angry self usually assumes. Instead, it started to dawn on me that the conditions that caused my anger to grow were internal, not external. My anger was my internal reaction to what happened to me. Instead of focusing on the external object of my anger, I was given a chance to know my own mind. And that 180-degree turn made all the difference. It was an essential component in my own dignity training.

Our typical mental habit is to ask why these things happen to us and why we feel sadness, anger, and fear. This conventional approach, unfortunately, does not take us very far in clearly and truthfully seeing ourselves and others. Instead, we are busy focusing on our projections, which often arise from a broken internal image. The question "why" keeps us occupied with those projections and images and with the narratives and fantasies they generate. This leaves us no hope of coming to know ourselves as we truly are.

Often, the appearance of an emotion such as anger is a way to forget our deep-seated low self-esteem, which ironically often disguises itself as pride. Pridefulness and low self-esteem alternate, or even fluctuate, with great instability. On the surface, a prideful person may seem strong and tough. In actuality, pride is a vulnerability, not a strength. When we cling to the appearances of anger or pride, we create our own theater and get caught up in our own illusory stories. It is as if we are watching a movie while falsely believing that the plot and its characters are real.

When I cried out to Nyoshul Khen Rinpoche, "I am angry," I explicitly identified with my anger. As a result, my anger actually worsened. By giving my anger an identity, I created a delusion. In truth, I am not anger, and anger is not me. Am I angry twenty-four hours a day? No. Of course not. I am much more than my anger. Then, "who" is angry? Or, in other words, "Who is 'I'?"

Deeply affected by Nyoshul Khen Rinpoche's questions, I realized that I habitually look outside myself to understand and deal with suffering that is actually of my own making. The key is to look inside, to examine how my mind is reacting to whatever is happening on the outside. That is how we begin to genuinely know ourselves. When I learned to develop dignity from my teachers by looking inward, my low self-esteem became an object of mindfulness. In the past, my low self-esteem was a disease. Now, it is a reminder for me to change.

Present Motivation, Future Aspirations

Nyoshul Khen Rinpoche was a very humble person. He escaped the Chinese occupation of his homeland, Tibet, at age twenty-seven, in a group of about seventy people; only five survived. He spent the following twenty-five years in India, alone and poverty-stricken. No one knew him. Later, Nyoshul Khen Rinpoche was recognized and revered as an extraordinary meditation master and learned scholar, teaching many young Tibetan lamas in India and Bhutan. But when he was not teaching, he would sit below the monks and nuns like an ordinary person. His humility was exemplary. Not being recognized by others did not humiliate him. The high status of a realized master did not make him prideful. He was always gentle, always steady and solid, never shaken by anything.

Being in the presence of people like my grandfather Tulku Urgyen Rinpoche and my teacher Nyoshul Khen Rinpoche taught me so much about dignity. In both their words and their actions, dignity shone through.

In my case, the teachings I received from these and other great masters came most alive when I experienced emotional turmoil. I experienced anger thousands of times. Anger is like morphine. You may feel good for a few hours, but after the morphine wears off you feel the pain again, sometimes with heightened intensity. When I reflect on these experiences now, I can see how I have changed, and I laugh at my earlier self for having created emotions that upset me.

Today both Tulku Urgyen Rinpoche and Nyoshul Khen Rinpoche are no longer physically here. But they continue to teach me and all others who are inspired by them. On one level, these masters inspire us to emulate them, as though we can mimic what they have done. At a deeper level, they inspire us because their qualities resonate with our own inner qualities. In them, we sense intuitively what is possible for us. We see that, like them, we can be vibrantly alive, effective, powerful human beings, and embody the qualities of compassion, wisdom, and dignity.

To be like these great masters, we cannot simply will ourselves to be like them. We need to cultivate the qualities they possess. To cultivate the qualities of compassion, wisdom, and dignity, we need to check our motivation and make aspirations. Motivation is like a mirror—it reflects your present intention. Aspiration is like a doorway to the future—it ushers you to the results you wish to achieve. Without motivation, you cannot even start on the path; without aspiration, it would be difficult to reach the result.

When I visited Nyoshul Khen Rinpoche in Bhutan many years ago, he gave me a teaching on five different levels of motivation. He spread the five fingers of his open hand as a visual representation.

"The first level of motivation is like my pinky finger," he said. In Tibetan culture, the pinky finger is associated with something very low. The lowest motivation for spiritual practice is wanting to be free from fear while enjoying worldly success and pleasure. Of course, when we are sick, we want to be well. When we are stressed, we want to relax. Whenever we have anything negative in our lives, we want to be rid of it. We want good health, and we want a long life of pleasurable experiences. The problem with this level of motivation is that it keeps our focus on the mundane and not the spiritual. We will remain distracted by pleasure throughout our lives and not achieve anything meaningful or lasting.

"The second level is neutral motivation." Nyoshul Khen Rinpoche pointed to his ring finger. It is neither positive nor negative, neither virtuous nor nonvirtuous. For example, when friends invite you to contribute to a charity, you say, "Why not, I'll just do as my friends do." Although you do something positive, you do it out of social influence or pressure rather than actual good intention.

The third level, represented by the middle finger, is being driven by fear. You avoid non-virtuous actions because you are afraid you will be punished for them. Now at least you are thinking about whether your actions are positive or negative, but you are still focused on their effect on you rather than on others.

The fourth level is called the motivation of self-liberation, symbolized by the index finger. You not only want to avoid doing wrong, but you also want to be liberated from all negative thought, emotion, and action. The focus is still subtly on yourself, but with the intention to remove that focus and achieve freedom.

Nyoshul Khen Rinpoche gave a thumbs-up when he elaborated on the fifth motivation—the motivation of *bodhicitta*. Bodhicitta is the sincere wish from deep in one's heart that all beings—without exception—attain the state of perfect enlightenment, meaning complete freedom from suffering and its causes. Now we take the focus away from ourselves alone and extend it to everyone.

After giving the teaching, Nyoshul Khen Rinpoche looked at me and asked, "Of these five, which motivation should we have?"

As Nyoshul Khen Rinpoche put it, the fifth motivation—the motivation of bodhicitta—is the supreme motivation. Bodhicitta is a Sanskrit word. *Bodhi* is usually translated as "awaken" and *citta* as "heart" or "mind." To have the motivation of bodhicitta—"the awakened heart"—is to have both understanding and compassion. We understand that all beings are connected with us, and that they suffer just as we do. Utilizing this connection, we sincerely and compassionately wish an end to all that suffering, as well as its causes. When we combine understanding and compassion, we naturally wish that all beings attain enlightenment, just like the Buddha. The motivation of bodhicitta is to transform ourselves through our practice so that we can help others, not only ourselves.

What is your motivation for wanting to learn about dignity? Of the five motivations described by Nyoshul Khen Rinpoche, which one do you have right now? For example, do you aspire to be a wealthy person? Which finger is that? What would be a higher aspiration? Don't judge or look down on yourself if your motivation is simply to be free from pain or stress. That's quite all right. It's good to be honest with yourself and acknowledge where you are. Just as it takes time to become a buddha or a mahasiddha, it takes time to develop motivation beyond self-interest. The key is to check yourself and know who you are right here and right now.

Your motivation will change when you gain more experience in knowing your own mind. In addition to reflecting on what motivates us now, it is important to keep in mind our future aspirations. Students in Asia told me that a common essay assignment for children is to answer the question "What do you want to be when you grow up?" Most students will write about wanting to be a physician, a firefighter, a teacher, an astronaut, and so forth. Making aspiration is a similar exercise, except that instead of focusing on a future career, and "what I want," we aspire to awakened qualities that go beyond mere self-interest. Aspiration is a wish of the heart, a lamp that illuminates the deep purpose of life.

Many buddhas and great masters who followed in the footsteps of the Buddha made extraordinary aspirations, such as wishing that all beings without exception be free from suffering and its causes. One inspiring example is Tara, the female buddha famously known as the "one who liberates." In a previous lifetime, recognizing that most buddhas are male, she made the fervent aspiration to always be reborn in female form. In paintings, Tara is frequently depicted as having one leg outstretched as if ready to leap to the assistance of anyone who is suffering. Her aspiration is powerful and inspiring.

Let me use an analogy to illustrate the importance of aspiration. Without aspiration, we are like a blind person trying to shoot an arrow at a target. Because we are blind, we cannot see where the target is. Aspiration is like the eyesight that enables us to aim the arrow. It directs us to our goal. Aspiration and motivation are necessary if we are to awaken and lead a meaningful life.

———————— DIGNITY TRAINING ————————

Making Aspiration

Take a quiet moment alone and ask yourself about your highest aspirations. To help you in this process, here are some different aspects for you to consider.

> Reflect on who your role models are. We need to be very careful about the role models we choose.
> What are the qualities of your role models?
> What would you have to do to become like them?
> What are your aspirations? You can begin each aspiration with "May I" to indicate your deep desire and dream—the purpose of life that you envision.
> What obstacles will your aspiration encounter—for example, not enough confidence in yourself, lack of discipline, not being sure how to make the aspiration a reality?

Again, this exercise is for you alone. Not judging yourself is the key. When we activate our aspiration consciously and continuously, it will change and grow. Through the dignity training in this book, you may find that your aspiration— your deep desire, your dream—changes.

Inspirational Support

> May I be a guard for those without one,
> A guide for all who journey on the road,
> May I become a boat, a raft or bridge,
> For all who wish to cross the water.
>
> May I be an isle for those desiring landfall,
> And a lamp for those who wish for light,
> May I be a bed for those who need to rest,
> And a servant for all who live in need.
>
> May I become a wishing jewel, a magic vase,
> A powerful mantra and a medicine of wonder.
> May I be a tree of miracles granting every wish,
> And a cow of plenty sustaining all the world.
>
> Like the earth and other great elements,
> And like space itself, may I remain forever,
> To support the lives of boundless beings,
> By providing all that they might need.
>
> Just so, in all the realms of beings,
> As far as space itself pervades,
> May I be a source of all that life requires,
> Until beings pass beyond saṃsara's pain.

SHANTIDEVA[1]

3

Beyond the Beautiful and the Ugly

Sentient beings are truly Buddhas
And yet are stained by adventitious obscurations.
When these are removed, indeed they're truly Buddhas.

LONGCHENPA[1]

Why do some people seem good and others bad? Are some people benevolent by nature and others inherently evil? Or maybe that is too simple. Are all people a mixture of good and bad elements? After all, even those we are closest to sometimes say or do unkind things, while our greatest enemies often possess undeniably good qualities. Confusing, right?

If other people are confusing to us, how do we perceive ourselves? You may ask yourself, "Am I good, or am I bad?" Maybe you've been told both in your life. I have heard it is common in Western cultures for parents to scold their children by saying, "Bad girl!" or "Bad boy!" That sounds painful. Of course, it is important to teach children right from wrong, or that they have done something they shouldn't, but that is very different from telling them they are "bad." When you receive a message like that from the most important person in your world, it tends to stick. No wonder so many people don't trust themselves and are plagued with self-doubt.

A favorite story of mine that relates to this issue comes from the *Tathagatagarbha Sutra*. I first learned it from a friend who is a professor of Buddhist studies. The story goes as follows. One day, the Buddha's students were looking at a field of lotus flowers. They perceived some of the flowers to be withered and ugly while others looked healthy and beautiful. Looking more closely, they noticed with delight that the beautiful lotuses had buddhas inside. But then they were surprised—even a little shocked—to discover that the ugly lotuses also had buddhas inside. One student voiced what all of them were thinking, saying to the Buddha, "It is easy to understand why the beautiful lotuses all have buddhas inside. But why do the ugly lotuses also have buddhas?"

The Buddha replied, "The outward appearance of the lotuses is like our character. Inwardly, everyone's basic nature is pure."

I should note that the "beauty" or "ugliness" of the lotus flowers has nothing to do with societal standards of attractiveness. Those with virtuous characters manifest as healthy and beautiful, like the pretty lotuses. But those whose characters are dominated by negative habits and qualities—what Buddhism calls *kleshas* or defilements—manifest the qualities of a mind that has grown withered and ugly. Even so, whatever our outward appearance, our deep-down basic nature is the same. In this story, the buddha at the heart of each lotus flower is a metaphor for the basic goodness of our own heart. Regardless of the character that encases it, our heart is pure, clean, and free of faults. This applies to each of us without exception, and it bears repetition and remembering: *Our nature is pure, my nature is pure, your nature is pure.*

Most Buddhists are familiar with the inspiring metaphor of the lotus flower that rises out of the mud only to stand above it, pure, beautiful, and unsoiled. The teaching of ugly lotuses is less known, but it really speaks to me. The image of an ugly, withered flower with a brilliant buddha abiding amid its petals affirms the fundamental goodness of our hearts. Some people have more compassion than others. Some people are more emotional than others. Some are prone to anger, and some to jealousy. Human beings have countless different personalities and characters. But regardless of our personalities or characters, on the level of our fundamental nature, we are all the same. We all have basic goodness. We all have within us the essence of awakening or enlightenment. Accordingly, we are not patently defective, as we sometimes believe; we are inherently noble. We might not always remember this. But the buddha in us knows that we are perfect.

Let me stress, again, that in this story, the words "ugly" and "beautiful" don't refer to socially and culturally conditioned judgments regarding age or outward appearance. The objects of our senses are not inherently beautiful or ugly apart from how we interpret them. What makes a lotus "ugly" or "beautiful" are the mental qualities that either align with our genuine nature or suppress it. The ugly lotus flowers reflect a mind habituated to negative emotions such as anger, jealousy, and greed. These negative emotions are called "poisons" because they are not natural. They disturb our mental state and create suffering for ourselves and for others. We all know these emotions, don't we? When we apply them repetitively in response to certain circumstances, they become habits. We sometimes become so habituated to various emotional patterns that we see life predominantly through their lens. For example, when we are chronically depressed, everything is depressing. When we are angry, other people are seen as threatening and become objects of our anger.

The good news is that our negative mental habits are temporary. They can change. But our nature underneath is pure and unchanging—this is the buddha in the lotus. Our true nature always shines, unhindered by whatever might obscure it. Buddhists call this nature "buddha-nature." The word "buddha" here does not refer to a person. It refers to the pure nature. Describing it as "pure" means it is free from mental confusion or obscurations.

What does the knowledge that our nature is pure do for those of us who were once admonished for being a "bad girl" or a "bad boy"? It offers us a new vision for ourselves, one that is deeply healing. We all have a good heart. We all have basic goodness. And our good heart is the foundation upon which we can reshape our sense of who we are. This is the foundation of our vajra pride, our dignity. When we have self-doubt, we have forgotten our good heart, and we lose our sense of dignity. When we remember our good heart, our sense of dignity is restored. We must always remember that we are good, even though we do make mistakes. Being inherently good and making mistakes are not contradictory. Mistakes merely reflect that we are in a process of becoming who we already are; mistakes do not and cannot affect our pure nature.

The World You Carry within Yourself

In my teaching tours, I have learned that many people easily identify with their personality or character yet have difficulty believing in their buddha-nature. They are strongly habituated to patterns of negative thinking combined with emotions such as anger, jealousy, anxiety, and dissatisfaction. These robust patterns are so pervasive that they scarcely recognize them, and when they do, they wholly identify with them. "This is just who I am," they might insist. Qualities of compassion, wisdom, and dignity remain mostly hidden, though they do arise fleetingly and come and go mysteriously. These individuals feel alienated from their good inner qualities, which necessarily means they are alienated from themselves. But, of course, their pure nature is always there, and it cannot be entirely suppressed. Many people are eager to learn how they can change, how they can improve themselves, what they can do to become better, stronger, and happier. Where does that come from? Our pure nature!

We are all shaped by our environments—family, culture, society, religion, and so on—yet at the same time we are individuals even before our environment shapes us. We each have our own patterns of thought, emotion, habit, and behavior. In other words, we have our own character and personality, or what we might call our "psychological self." Some people are easily irritable while others are naturally patient. Some people are short-tempered while others are naturally gentle and sweet. By the time we become adults, we bear the burden of trying to synthesize the expectations and demands of our family, society, and culture with our own sense of being a unique individual. It is very difficult to do!

A student named Jimmy runs a healing program in Indonesia called Dharmajala. The program reflects an effort to apply Buddhist teachings to alleviate contemporary social, political, and environmental injustice and suffering. According to Jimmy's research and field experience, much of the suffering individuals go through reflects the accumulation of their earlier life experiences. Many people nationwide experience difficult childhoods with abusive or neglectful parents. These individuals might seek out friends or companions for support, but many of these companions are dealing with their own hurts and wounds, so their counsel often only serves to make things worse. Alternatively, some seek support from community centers, churches or temples, spiritual teachers, or even gangs. Some find solace in these communities while others do not. Jimmy's aspiration is to provide support to those who struggle with individual, family, and community crises and offer tools for them to be their "own therapists."

It is useful to have some knowledge of how we are shaped by our family and society and to know how we each are born with certain personalities. Knowing our psychological self is undoubtedly important. In the process, however, we sometime forget about our spiritual self. Without knowing the difference between our character and our nature, and without knowing that our nature is pure, change could be very limited. On the other hand, if we know that our nature is pure, the mistakes we make, the challenges we face, and the anxiety and doubt in our mind can give us great encouragement for change. When we know that our nature is pure, change is not only possible—it is desirable. Jimmy's program has been helpful to the people of Indonesia because it integrates the psychological with the spiritual rather than focusing on one at the exclusion of the other.

If we despise ourselves and believe that we are defective, there is little room for us to change and improve. If we don't recognize our good heart, it is hard to benefit ourselves or others. In Buddhism, the emotional defilements manifesting in our character are believed to be adventitious, meaning they are not intrinsic to who we are—they can change. They are like the clouds in the sky. The sky is not affected by the clouds floating by. The sky is always there and always the same, whether we have a clear view of it or not. Similarly, our buddha-nature is not affected by our negative habitual patterns. It is always there and always the same, whether our negative habitual patterns obstruct it or not. Therefore, our task is to see beyond that which obscures our original purity and connect with it directly.

The bottom line is that we are not our characters. We may have long been carrying a broken world inside us, but this is just an entrenched habit of mind. It is not who we are. If we focus solely on our psychological self, we will never live up to the expectations that society creates for us, and we will always feel angry that the world is not perfect and that we are defective. Then we will see the world in terms of self and other, right and wrong. This kind of dualistic thinking results when we are distracted from our nature—we have forgotten who we truly are.

Mind and Its Nature

The entire Buddhist path can be divided into two categories: mind and its nature. Even though these are separate categories, the mind is of course inseparable from its nature, in the same way that a wave is inseparable from the ocean. In Buddhism, "mind" refers to the thoughts, emotions, and sensations that pass through our conscious awareness. The "nature of mind" is the awareness itself. You see, it really is like the wave and the ocean. It is quite simple and logical, isn't it?

If we want to take in a view of the ocean, we must stop playing in the waves and get a larger view. Similarly, if we want to become aware of our true nature, we must stop identifying with the constant stream of activity in our mind and adopt a larger view. Why? As we have seen, we tend to think this activity is who we are. So long as we swim in our mind's waves, we will never experience its vastness and depth. To gain this larger perspective, we must learn to know our mind.

Learning to know our mind requires that we stop seeing ourselves as deficient. Ironically, doing that requires that we examine our faults so that we can address and overcome them. But this is difficult, right? If we feel deficient, how are we going to take an honest look at our negative habitual patterns? It can be quite scary, terrifying even. Therefore, it is helpful to remember, yet again: *Your nature is pure.* You are not your faults. This reassurance might help nudge us to look, and eventually the benefit we experience from looking will encourage us to keep going. Now we are getting to know our mind.

In this process of knowing our mind, one of the most important questions we must ask ourselves is how kind we are. But first, we must know what kindness is.

"Is kindness self-love?"

A young man raised this question after a talk I gave in the United Kingdom.

"Yes and no," I said. "Kindness is love, but it is love without focus on self. Kindness is love and care without ego."

Kindness is one of the most basic, positive qualities that we all share as living, breathing beings. It is not an idea. It is an experience of goodness in ourselves and others.

If we create an artificial distinction between self and other, then the kindness, or love, disappears. You have a mind, and I have a mind, and their nature is the same. This is our mutual ground. It doesn't matter how we look, speak, or think. Our nature does not have a passport. A British person has a British passport, and someone born in Nepal, like me, has a Nepali passport. There we do make a distinction. But not for the nature of mind. A passport has a photo of a face that changes over time. A passport has the name that was arbitrarily given to you. How your face looks at a moment in time is not your nature. And your name is not your nature.

The Buddha taught that all beings have buddha-nature, which is the basis of loving-kindness, wisdom, and dignity. Knowing this is also the basis for recognizing that everyone is equal. And it is the basis for true dignity. If we don't know that other people have the same nature as we do, then we might not respect them. We will always make comparisons and think that others are either superior or inferior to us. This kind of comparison game prevents us from knowing our mind—its weaknesses and strengths—and distracts us from our nature.

Cultivating dignity requires that we see how strong and powerful this mind is but also how fragile it is. The mind is the most powerful determinant of our experience because it can change happiness into sadness, and sadness into happiness, in a split second. But when such change happens suddenly without our control, our state of mind becomes very fragile. We might compensate by trying to make our mind strong, but instead it becomes rigid, like a board. We might be attached to our passport photo that was taken five years earlier, thinking that's how we look today. The reality is that we don't look exactly like that anymore. We are always changing, and our experience is always changing.

Our feelings change, our emotions change, conditions change, and our bodies change. Our perceptions change as well. It is important to keep our mind from becoming rigid. We must keep our mind supple, flexible, and steady. Otherwise, we will be vulnerable to many ups and downs in the face of external conditions.

It is helpful to have some familiarity with the topic of buddha-nature. Without at least an intellectual understanding of the nature of mind, it is very challenging to cultivate dignity and really experience it. Again, buddha-nature has nothing to do with being Buddhist. It is simply our awakened nature. All beings with minds—often referred to as "sentient beings"—have the same basic buddha-nature. This includes not only human beings and animals, but even beings that we can't see with our limited sensory systems.

Buddha-nature itself is often compared with space because it is vast and expansive. And it is often said in the Buddhist tradition, "As far as space pervades, there are sentient beings." Because these sentient beings all have buddha-nature, buddha-nature pervades everywhere. It is always with us, but we are unaware of it. Why don't we recognize it? Why is a fish unaware that it swims in water? We often overlook the natural environment in which we swim, or in our case, move. For example, we usually don't notice the air we breathe until there is a problem. Human beings are fortunate to have the intelligence to discover air and study it. Similarly, we are fortunate to have the intelligence to discover buddha-nature and realize it.

Why is it so important to discover our buddha-nature? We must know our pure, inherent nature if we want to be fully grounded. When we have returned to our primordial ground, we won't disturb our own mind or the minds of others. We will no longer be following ideas of who we should be; we will simply be who we really are and have always been. How do we do this? It is very straightforward: we must come to know both our mind and our mind's nature.

Getting to Know Our Mind

The first step in the process of knowing our mind and its nature is to know our mind's current state—to know what thoughts and emotions are preventing us from being content and happy. Coming to know ourselves in this way is important. But just knowing it does not make the confusion go away.

Next, we must apply methods to liberate our mind's confusion. Once that confusion is gone, the mind's wisdom naturally shines and the qualities of emptiness, clarity, and compassion are naturally present. The absence of confusion is the awakened state. There is a common way of expressing this in Buddhism: When we recognize our own innate nature, we are a buddha. When we do not recognize it, we are a sentient being.

Knowing that our nature is pure gives us a deep and abiding sense of security, no matter what kind of chaos might be happening in our environment. This deep sense of security provides a firm foundation upon which we can activate our motivation to benefit others. It also provides fuel for that motivation. Knowing that we and everyone else have the same pure nature, and recognizing how wonderful that pure nature is, we are naturally moved to help others to see this for themselves.

Unfortunately, we do not always believe that our nature is pure, good, and beautiful. Perhaps we do sometimes. But when life's difficulties bring up negative thoughts and feelings, we tend to fall back on our habitually low opinion of ourselves. In those moments, we forget who we really are. We feel a different sense of security, the security we place in the ideas and emotions we use to distract ourselves from how we really feel. To put it another way, we find a certain comfort in the familiarity of our discomfort. This obviously is not a good long-term strategy if we want genuine happiness. To bring long-lasting happiness and stable dignity, we need to develop a new skill. And this begins with a new view of ourselves and others.

——————— DIGNITY TRAINING ———————

A New Mantra

Things we say repeatedly throughout the course of our everyday lives shape who we are. Ordinarily we don't pay any attention to the constant chatter going on in our minds. What kinds of things do you repeat to yourself every day? Do these messages help you to be more open, loving, and wise toward yourself and others? Or do they create fear and apprehension or perhaps anger, craving, jealousy, or arrogance? Check yourself. If what you repeat in your mind over and over inhibits your love, compassion, wisdom, and dignity, then it's time to develop a new habit, a new skill.

We can do this by reciting a mantra in place of our usual mental chatter, much of which is based on the negative ideas we hold about ourselves. The principle of reciting a mantra is no different from any other new skill we develop, whether learning to speak Mandarin Chinese or play the piano. We must practice repeatedly. Mastering any new skill requires endless repetition, so why should transforming our mind be any different?

In the Buddhist tradition, mantras are recited to protect the mind from falling into negativity. Mantra is a Sanskrit word combining *manas*, meaning "mind," and *tra*, meaning "protect." So mantra means "protector of the mind." What does the mind need protection from? Negative thoughts and emotions. My grandfather Tulku Urgyen Rinpoche once said, "When we are chanting mantras, we are not saying anything negative." In other words, chanting mantras is a way to effectively counter our habitual tendency of speaking in negative terms. When our mantra conveys a positive message, then we are replacing a negative message with a positive one.

Usually, we chant or recite a particular mantra many times. Therefore, mantra also implies repetition. The mantras that Buddhist practitioners recite usually consist of sacred syllables. They are considered sacred because they carry the enlightened energy of all the highly realized practitioners who have recited them in the past. When we recite sacred mantras, we resonate with the same vibratory energy as countless enlightened beings.

But the mantra we chant doesn't have to be in Sanskrit or come from a specific tradition. Most important is that it has an intentional meaning and purpose. For example, we can develop a mantra for the purpose of constantly reminding ourselves of our innermost intentions and true nature. Then we can chant this mantra anywhere, any time—when we walk, when we cook, when we wash dishes, when we drive, when we ride on an airplane. In this way, we protect our mind from forgetting and lapsing back into its habitual patterns of negative thinking and strong emotions.

You can begin this practice by saying the following mantra: *The nature of my mind is pure; the nature of all beings is pure.*

Chanting mantras is a simple but powerful practice. It is a form of meditation that protects you from being distracted. It is also a form of prayer, aspiration, and purification. Chanting mantras is mindfulness. Above all, chanting mantras is a method that can bring you to the realization of your deepest nature.

If you did not believe that your nature is pure, you would be missing the essence of your dignity—the nature of who you are. The next time you notice a negative self-narrative, such as "I am not good enough," "I hate myself," or "I am stupid," try to gently come back to your new mantra. Remind yourself and repeat again and again: "The nature of my mind is pure; the nature of all beings is pure." After practicing like this for a while, gently bring awareness to what you experience. Do you see that your character (ruled by habits) and your nature (the essence of who you are) are not the same thing? You may start to see that when your mind is not preoccupied with putting yourself (or others) down, you experience a little bit of clarity, freshness, and openness in your heart. Try it and see for yourself.

Inspirational Support

> Whatever we see, we think it is seen through the eyes, but actually it is seen through the power of unobstructed, stainless awareness mind.
>
> Whatever we hear, we think it is heard through the ears, but actually it is heard through the power of unobstructed, stainless awareness mind.
>
> Whatever we smell, we think it is smelled through the nose, but actually it is smelled through the power of unobstructed, stainless awareness mind.
>
> Whatever we taste, we think it is tasted through the tongue, but actually it is tasted through the power of unobstructed, stainless awareness mind.
>
> Whatever we feel, we think it is felt through touch, but actually it is felt through the power of unobstructed, stainless awareness mind.
>
> THINLEY NORBU RINPOCHE[2]

4

Three Meditation Teachers

I have shown you the path to liberation.
But liberation depends on you alone.
THE BUDDHA[1]

Now that we appreciate our nature is pure—that we are the buddha in the lotus—we can start to go beyond intellectual understanding to cultivate a living experience of this nature. It is by directly recognizing our nature that we create the conditions to live a dignified life. How do we do this? Through meditation. Learning to meditate properly requires the assistance of three teachers. The first is the human teacher who shows us the way, and the other two are inner guides who help us along the way.

Human Teacher: Spiritual Friend

The role of the human teacher is to remind us about our mind and its nature. In the Tibetan Buddhist tradition, the teacher is regarded as a "spiritual friend," one who has gone through the journey and is able to guide us when we travel to unknown places. Imagine you are crossing a wide ocean with no one steering the boat or dealing with the wind, waves, or dangerous currents. The ocean is so vast that without a captain you would get lost and never reach your destination. Similarly, our mind is like a vast ocean upon which we must find our way. The captain for our journey is our spiritual friend, and the boat that will bring us home is our friend's teachings on the mind. This teacher is very familiar with both the "boat" and the "ocean" and can guide us to recognize our mind, its activities, its nature, and its inherent qualities.

My first teachers, including my grandfather and Nyoshul Khen Rinpoche, never told me what to do to develop dignity. Instead, they showed me a path that I had to explore myself. My grandfather taught that no matter how many teachings we receive, neither the teachings nor the teachers will solve our problems; real change comes only from the direct experience we gain through practicing the teachings. He used an analogy to stress how important direct experience is in our journey of awakening. He said:

We can look at a plate of food and imagine what it tastes like. And we can think, "Mmm, I am eating the food. I am no longer hungry." We can do this for a long time, but so long as it remains imaginary, it will not alleviate our hunger. The only way to relieve hunger is to put food in your mouth!

Then my grandfather emphasized: "Experience only occurs in a direct way, in practical reality, not through a theory about taste." In other words, while intellect is important, it is not enough to cultivate our dignity. We must meditate. Knowledge about our mind has little power itself to transform our anger or depression.

Because the human teacher can only show us the path, leaving us to do the work ourselves, we need additional guidance when we're sitting on our meditation cushion. My teachers explained to me that there are two other kinds of teachers on whom we should rely. These are the inner teacher and the ultimate teacher. The human teacher points us in the right direction, and then we use the guidance that comes directly out of our personal experience to go the distance.

Inner Teacher: Mindfulness

Our second teacher, the inner teacher, is mindfulness. Mindfulness is the best gift we can give to ourselves and to others. At one level, mindfulness means "recollecting." We recollect, or recall, what it is we are supposed to be doing. At another level, mindfulness refers to an awareness of what is happening in the moment. Thus, mindfulness acts like a pillar that roots us in our immediate lived experience. With mindfulness, we know the state of our mind. We see clearly which activities trigger our emotions and disturb us. With mindfulness, we can remind ourselves to transform our mental behavior and continually deepen and expand our inherent good qualities. Mindfulness is the tool by which we can stabilize our recognition of the state of our mind, its activities, its nature, and its inherent qualities.

Ultimate Teacher: Nature of Mind

The third teacher, the ultimate teacher, goes beyond mindfulness. It is the nature of mind itself, our true home, and the basis of dignity. What is the nature of mind? It is open, vast, unchanging awareness rich with the qualities of love, compassion, and wisdom. This awareness is always present, even though our absorption in thoughts, emotions, and sensations usually obscures it. Because awareness is always present, it continually operates under the surface, guiding us to do the right thing. For example, there are times when we are tempted to do something, and maybe we can't come up with a good reason not to, but deep down we know that it is wrong. We have an intuitive knowing, an inner wisdom that guides us. It is in this sense that awareness, our mind's nature, is the ultimate teacher.

As I mentioned earlier, when Siddhartha Gautama achieved enlightenment to become the Buddha, he realized that this unchanging awareness, or buddha-nature, is present in everyone. It is who (or what) we really are. It remains latent in us in the same way that butter is latent in milk. If I give you milk, you won't see the butter, initially. But if you shake the milk—really shake, shake, shake it—then butter will start to show. When we work to transform our ordinary mind of thoughts and emotions, the mind's genuine nature starts to reveal itself, including its inherent qualities of love, compassion, and wisdom. This nature is the buddha in the heart of our lotus, the perfection that we already are, and the deep source of our interest in the spiritual path. This is our ultimate teacher.

Earlier, when I said that the role of the teacher is to remind us about our mind and its nature, you probably thought I only meant the human teacher. But I could have been speaking about any of the three. In fact, these three teachers are inseparable. The first teacher, the human teacher, is not teaching anything external or foreign to us. The purpose of this teacher is simply to show us our mind, its basic nature, and how to be in touch with it. In this way, we come to understand and appreciate the perfect, fully awakened nature always present in us. The second teacher, mindfulness, reminds us to remain in contact with this nature. Through mindfulness, we attend to how our mind is doing. Is the mind peaceful or disturbed? Which activities trigger it? What are our mental habits? How can we transform them? The capacity of mindfulness is already in us. The third teacher, nature of mind, is our true home, the fruition of our path as well as its driving force. It constantly calls us home.

Learning to Meditate

Seeing the inseparability of the three teachers in this way is the basis of meditation and transformation: after recognizing our mind's nature with the help of our first (human) teacher, our second teacher (mindfulness) keeps us in contact with it, while our third teacher (mind's nature) reveals to us its riches. When we can recognize and maintain our true nature with certainty, we have dignity, and this dignity expresses itself in our lives effortlessly. We are grounded in a genuine nature from which we had previously lost contact, but from which we have never ultimately been separated. Therefore, true dignity is not something we learn in a classroom or from reading a book. It must be experienced and embodied.

To experience and embody our dignity, we must come to know both our lotus and our inner buddha. We must know our character and its habitual patterns and recognize that these are not who we genuinely are. We must come to know that our nature is pure and gain experience and confidence in that.

We may be able to see, from time to time, that we are unhappy, dissatisfied, anxious, or angry. Attending to these feelings reflects an early expression of awareness. It can make us uncomfortable to see our own "ugly lotus," but doing so holds tremendous potential for transformation. Remember, our actual nature is pure. Encouraged by this realization, we can summon the courage to examine whatever is arising in our mind—without judgment and with mindfulness. If we have mindfulness, we will see that the energy that gives rise to anger and other negative emotions has wisdom, and that the underlying sense of insecurity we feel is not necessarily a bad thing.

With training and practice, mindfulness can bring us back to our true home—our fundamental, unchanging goodness—our innate, ultimate teacher. What the three teachers teach is how to become the master of our own mind, how to cease being the slave of our character. Everyone can practice it and experience its results.

Because some of our habits are extremely strong, it may take a while to loosen their control over us to relax in our inner dignity, rooted in our natural wisdom mind. I encourage you to take your time and proceed gradually. The following dignity training meditation is designed to help you take these small steps to becoming free from the habitual patterns that trouble you. Eventually you will become steadfast in the face of whatever circumstances you encounter.

DIGNITY TRAINING

Meditation Posture

As you follow the training, it is important to keep in mind that dignity is not a possession or another goal to achieve in life. The sole purpose of dignity training is to empower what we already have—to stabilize our best human qualities so that we can be the wisdom that knows, the compassion that loves and cares, and the power that protects and benefits ourselves and others.

There is a pithy way to think about the relationship between body and mind in meditation:

Body on the cushion.
Mind in the body.
Mind at rest.

Meditation is only one of many methods to develop dignity. But because it is the primary doorway to knowing our mind and reconnecting with our intrinsic, pure nature, meditation is indispensable in dignity training. As introduced earlier, meditation should be preceded by contemplation and reflection on our basic character, our motivation, and our aspiration.

In Tibetan, the word for meditation is *gom*, meaning "to become familiar with."

Meditation helps us become familiar with who we really are, to recognize and remember that our nature is pure. No matter how many books we read or how many great teachings we receive, these are limited in helping us develop dignity. But through meditation, we can genuinely experience dignity from the bottom of our heart.

> Begin by sitting on a comfortable cushion or in a chair. Let your body relax with your spine straight but not tensed. Sitting straight allows the energy to flow more freely in the body, which sharpens your awareness.

> Your eyes can look forward, up, or down; they can move or blink when needed. In some traditions, practitioners close their eyes as an aid to calming the mind. The training here is about awakening and sharpening the mind. It is about awareness, not relaxation, so keeping your eyes open is best. If you find it too difficult to keep your eyes open, lowering your gaze might help.

> Your chin should be down a little bit, with your head always held in the same position.

> Open your mouth slightly so that you breathe through both your nose and your mouth.

> Let your breath flow naturally; do not control or alter your breathing.

> Your mind should stay in the body and not wander around to different places or times. If your body is in New York but your mind is in London, then you

are not meditating. The mind is easily distracted by memories of the past or plans for the future. When this happens, don't judge yourself—just gently bring the mind back to the body in the present moment.

When the mind is in the body, and the body is relaxed, the mind can rest in its natural state, a state that is inherently calm and clear. A key principle in meditation is to maintain balance so that the body and mind are neither too tight nor too loose. It is like archery, a sport I very much enjoy. To shoot arrows using a bow, one must remain still and concentrated, neither too tense nor too relaxed, aware but not uptight. It is by maintaining relaxed concentration that you can hit your target. You need some effort, but not too much, and you should never attach to the results.

Gentle Focus Meditation

> Once you assume a comfortable meditation posture, gently focus your attention on a chosen object or image. The object could be a flower, a stone, or the tip of a pen. The image could be a photo.
> It might be a challenge initially to not talk or move your body, but with time it will be easier to remain silent and still. If you notice that your mind has become distracted—whether by something external in your environment or, more commonly, by your own wandering thought process—that is wonderful. By noticing this, you have increased your awareness. Don't follow the distraction, but don't fight it either. Just gently bring your attention back to your chosen object of focus.
> Repeatedly bringing your mind back strengthens your mindfulness and concentration.

The purpose of this gentle focus meditation is to bring the calmness and clarity required to see your thoughts arising and dissolving. You become more aware of your thought processes and how they influence your speech and actions. This enhances your capacity for self-reflection and makes you less prone to judgment.

The value of gentle focus meditation is not in its length or how much relaxation occurs. The goal is a fresh and clear mind. So at the beginning, doing just a few minutes of meditation at a time and repeating it many times throughout the day will ensure faster progress. The combination of fresh moments and many times is especially beneficial for beginning meditators.

Inspirational Support

> To discipline your mind and have concentration you need to become your own teacher. A skillful teacher can give guidelines and instructions to assist you, but real discipline and concentration must come from yourself. External supports or forces cannot subdue your mind and bring you good concentration.
>
> KHENCHEN PALDEN SHERAB RINPOCHE AND
> KHENPO TSEWANG DONGYAL RINPOCHE[2]

Part Two

You Can Change

One who lacks self-guidance
And later possesses mindfulness
Is like a radiant moon being freed from clouds.

NĀGĀRJUNA[1]

5

Making Friends with "Sticky Mind"

Becoming "awake" involves seeing
our confusion more clearly.

CHÖGYAM TRUNGPA[1]

I have always enjoyed visiting Jackson Hole in Wyoming. A place of beautiful natural scenery, this is where I gave my first teaching after completing my formal studies in India. I have made many good friends in Jackson Hole over the years, and I try to stop there whenever I can. On my last visit, I had a nice lunch with friends at a restaurant in the picturesque Town Square. Afterward, I saw a beautiful dog outside the restaurant. It looked like a Siberian husky. Being fond of dogs, I wanted to find out if it really was a Siberian husky. So I asked the dog owner, "What is that?"

"It is a dog," the owner replied, rolling her eyes.

Realizing my question was not clear, I rephrased it: "What kind of dog is it?"

The owner shrugged and mumbled something I couldn't comprehend. Sensing that she was irritated and didn't care to have a conversation, I said, "Okay," and walked away.

When others don't respond positively to our friendly attempts at engaging them, we might simply notice this in a matter-of-fact way, thinking, "I was just trying to have a conversation, but she didn't want to." Or we might feel concern about the other person, thinking, "Poor thing, she must be having a bad day." Perhaps most common is that the experience ignites an emotional response in us: "She is so rude!" This last example would indicate that we are taking things personally and jumping to conclusions. This is very tempting for us to do, but the reality is often different from what we assume. What appears before our eyes rarely gives us the whole picture. Do we know why the dog owner was grumpy that day? Not at all, right? We must take her situation into account and recognize that we don't have all the information. In other words, we must try to look beneath the surface and not take things at face value.

But how many of us, when encountering a situation like this, have the time, mental space, and composure to mindfully respond in a deliberate and skillful way? Instead of a calm and open response, such situations often elicit an automatic and compulsive reaction. When our mind is calm and stable, we are happy and respond to situations calmly. When our mind is irritated and unstable, our feelings swing quickly, changing from happiness to sadness in an instant. Then we react in ways that we might later regret.

The next day, I was giving a teaching during a meditation retreat in the majestic Rocky Mountains. I told the retreat participants the story of my encounter with the dog owner. The moment I started talking, I knew I was not 100 percent free of the incident. In all honesty, the incident did not bother me or affect my mood; I went on with my day as if nothing had happened. But the fact that I remembered it and then told the story unveiled a very subtle form of clinging barely detectable yet lurking beneath my consciousness. I call this type of clinging "sticky mind."

Often sticky mind is not so subtle. Rather than simply recalling an incident, as I did in this case, we might ruminate and obsess over it. We might harshly judge another person and do or say things in a reactive and hurtful way. We might be plagued with self-doubt and find ourselves overtaken by a mood that is difficult to shake. It feels like something sticky has infected us, but that's not quite it. It is our mind that is sticky.

In a nutshell, *sticky mind is emotion stuck in concept.* Fixed ideas and negative emotions mutually support each other. Our feelings and emotions are constantly changing, but because of the sticky quality of our mind, we perceive them as permanent. Therefore, we tend to attach to things we like and avoid things we don't. These tendencies develop into habits, resulting in patterns or grooves in which our mind moves. We develop a narrow and constricted view of who we are and how the world is, and we interpret events in a way that fits this view. It feels as if the ideas, feelings, and perceptions associated with this way of seeing latch on to us and won't let go. In actuality, it is our mind that holds them close. It is our mind that is sticky. It is our mind that makes a dynamic reality static and fixed.

Viewing ourselves as static and fixed prevents us from knowing our genuine nature. It limits us and makes us inflexible. When our mind is sticky, we often act in ways that contradict our fundamental goodness or best intentions. Sticky mind prevents us from being fundamentally open, free, kind, and loving to ourselves and to others. It prevents us from knowing and embracing our inherent dignity.

What is the solution to sticky mind? How do we deal with emotion stuck in concept? Whether sticky mind is as subtle as remembering an unusual incident that recently happened or as coarse as obsessive rumination, I have found that simply being aware of my sticky mind gives me the power to change. The moment we glimpse our disturbing emotions and the concepts that support them, they begin to weaken. They cannot grow in the light of awareness. On the other hand, lack of awareness is fertile ground for afflictive emotions. When the right supporting conditions come together, negative emotions can erupt without warning, causing harm to others and to ourselves. Therefore, it is imperative that we come to know these negative emotions and see them whenever they arise. In time, the patterns that maintain them will weaken, and our minds won't be so adhesive.

The Emotions That Disturb the Mind

Buddhist texts provide a classification of the negative emotions that characterize the coarse forms of sticky mind. According to these texts, there are 84,000 such emotions. Fortunately, we can effectively address all of them by simply working with the five overarching categories into which they are summarized: anger, pride, jealousy, attachment, and ignorance. These states of mental confusion are also called the "five poisons" to convey how seriously they disturb our mind. When under the control of these poisons, we don't see reality clearly, and we don't see ourselves clearly. We have no wisdom.

As mentioned in chapter 3, the true nature of our mind is pure and spacious like the sky. Thoughts and feelings are like clouds simply passing by. They abide for a while but eventually disappear, leaving the sky untouched. But in our case, our sky often becomes overcast, sometimes stormy, because our emotions get stuck in the misguided ideas that we hold on to. The foremost problem is believing that we are a separate, permanent self, or "I." This misguided notion hooks us into fixating on whatever drama our mind creates, pitting our "I" against perceived enemies. The five poisons proliferate and thrive in such an environment. Then we have full-blown sticky mind.

It is therefore essential to become aware of these negative emotions and the thought patterns that support them. You might think we want to avoid or even destroy these emotions, but that only makes them bigger enemies and stronger opponents. The secret is to make friends with them. Through seeing them, hearing them, and understanding them, our negative emotions lose their power and transform into something entirely different. They become sources of wisdom rather than confusion.

Anger

I have a friend in Nepal who is very short-tempered. Troubled by his temper, he decided to participate in a one-week anger management course. Upon his return, he came to visit and told me how relaxed, peaceful, and calm he had been feeling. "The anger management really works," he said. As we were talking, a young monk brought us tea. While serving us, the monk tripped and spilled tea all over my friend's pants. My friend shouted at the monk, "Hey, what are you doing? See what you did!" Suddenly, his peaceful face had turned red, tinted with irritation. Then, in the blink of an eye, he turned toward me, smiling, as if nothing had happened. He didn't notice that he had just burst out in anger.

Often, it is easier to detect other people's problems than to see our own faults. This friend's anger was visible to me but not to him. However, some emotions are so subtle that even others cannot detect them. These emotions, including dislike and discomfort, are harder to uproot because they often stay buried deep in the mind and don't express themselves externally. But a few budding dislikes and discomforts continuing over time might change that. We might see this person suddenly explode in anger.

Anger is like a fire that burns us and those around us without discrimination. When we are angry, we usually think that someone or something external to us is responsible for our anger. This is not at all true. No matter what kinds of things happen or what people do, our negative reactions to them could not have manifested without an internal mental process involving our own perceptions and afflictions. In short, none of the external enemies we perceive would exist without our having created an internal enemy to oppose them.

Getting to know our mind is very important. When we lash out in anger, we stop seeing what is real and what is not. Anger obscures our ability to slow down and be mindful; it blinds us to the consequences of our actions. Let me use myself as an example. When I was in the shedra in India, a classmate told me that when I feel angry, rather than suppressing it, I should punch a wall. "Let the anger out," he said. And I did. But what I found was that the more I expressed any negative emotion, including anger, the more I reinforced it. Expressing anger did nothing to tackle its root cause. Without understanding my anger and its root cause, punching the wall did nothing to free me from it.

Pride

The feeling of pride is like having a comfortable scarf wrapped around our neck without realizing it is actually a poisonous snake that can bite us at any time. Pride—the comforting feeling that we are superior to others—is a self-sabotaging emotion. Prideful persons have a strong sense of "I" around which all their perceptions revolve, generating a strong sense of ownership and obsessiveness. When the prideful "I" is hurt, they feel victimized. This easily invites other negative emotions. When pride is present, jealousy, ignorance, and attachment appear easily.

It might take time to notice our pride and see its effects because it is more subtle and hidden than anger. Like anger, pride can be expressed in an external manner that is visible for all to see, such as when we say and do something clearly arrogant. But many of us are good at hiding our pride, keeping it internal and out of sight. To be able to transform pride, we must be honest with ourselves. The very thing that makes such honesty possible is what makes it difficult in the first place: acknowledging our pride requires a certain degree of humility. The acknowledgment itself is its own antidote.

Jealousy

Jealousy is a feeling of discomfort that arises in the face of other people's favorable circumstances or good fortune, such as their accomplishments, possessions, social status, good looks, or positive qualities. Jealousy can be expressed in many forms, including resentment, envy, fear, and desire. Although jealousy appears to be triggered by external factors, it can creep up and seize our mind at any moment, regardless of what is happening in our environment.

To put it simply, we are jealous of others when they possess something that we don't. Therefore, the root of jealousy is comparison. We see ourselves as separate from others, and we place our happiness higher than theirs. We compare and judge, generating complicated waves of emotion that revolve around wanting what we don't have while being jealous of those who have the very things we want. It is a painful experience! In addition to inviting unpleasant thoughts and stress, the worst part of jealousy is that it damages trust in our basic goodness.

Attachment

While jealousy focuses on what we don't have, attachment focuses on what we do have. With attachment, not only do we want to keep what we have, but we also want more of what we have. Both aspects of attachment are destructive. Emotionally clinging to what we have demonstrates insecurity; wanting more of what we have demonstrates dissatisfaction.

A pediatrician who attended one of my retreats was puzzled by the idea that attachment is a root destructive emotion. She explained that in Western developmental psychology, attachment is considered a critical emotional bond that infants need to establish with their mothers or primary caregivers. "The strength of this bond determines whether or not the child can later establish healthy relationships with others," she added. After listening to her, I told her there is no contradiction. That kind of bond between a parent and child is pure; it is a source of joy and freedom. What Buddhism generally refers to as "attachment" is different. Attachment is a desire based on clinging to or fixating on something or someone. This kind of mental attitude disturbs our inner peace and freedom, creating suffering. In a way, the Buddhist concept of attachment is comparable to obsession or addiction. When we are addicted to or obsessed with something or someone, we become slaves to our own attachments, powerless to free ourselves from them.

I was surprised the first time I saw a "shopping channel" on TV. It seemed its sole purpose was to manipulate our desire, tempting us to buy things we really don't need. If we are not careful, our usual mode of mind becomes "buying mind." When we buy one thing, we crave the second, then the third, the fourth, and so on. Soon we might find ourselves buying twenty pairs of shoes at once, even though we don't have twenty pairs of feet to wear them. Our "buying mind" lures us to purchase products as if we are planning to live for hundreds of years. This is how desire and attachment affect our mind—we never feel we have enough. The Buddha teaches that trying to satisfy our desires is like drinking salt water from the ocean to quench our thirst. The more we drink, the thirstier we become, and the greater the craving we generate. And then we get stuck in the vicious circle of wanting more and more without ever being satisfied. We have not yet learned where to seek genuine satisfaction.

Ignorance

Every negative emotion is the result of ignorance. The experience of ignorance is like living in darkness—we don't see what we are doing or what is going on around us. But it's even worse than that.

In ignorance, we're not even aware of the darkness itself. We don't know we're in darkness because we don't know there is light.

There are two basic types of ignorance, both of which are pervasive in almost everything we do. The first kind of ignorance functions like a blind spot. We don't notice everything that is happening in our field of experience, including our inner life and afflictive emotions. In this ignorance, we "ignore" or are blind to certain aspects of our experience. This ignorance is one of the five poisons alongside anger, jealousy, pride, and attachment.

The other form of ignorance is the deeper and more fundamental source of all five poisons. It is ignorance of our basic nature. We don't realize that our nature is pure. Consequently, we don't recognize that everything—all beings and their environments—are radically interconnected and interdependent. Instead, we view ourselves as a permanent, intrinsic self that is separate and apart from the world and all other beings in it. Although it is true that this is how things appear, we must look beneath the surface of appearances. Deep down this kind of subject-object duality is an illusion. Our basic nature is beyond duality. When we are ignorant of our basic nature, we live in darkness without knowing that we do.

The Greek philosopher Plato told an allegory about a group of prisoners who lived their whole lives chained to a wall in a cave. Day in and day out all they ever saw were shadows projected on the wall by a fire behind them. They could not turn around to see the fire, and so they thought these shadows were real objects; the play of light and dark had become the prisoners' reality. One day, when the prisoners were exposed to direct sunlight upon leaving the cave, they realized that the shadows were not real, that their notion of the real world had been an illusion.

As with the shadows in Plato's cave, we mostly live in an imagined reality that seems real to us but is an illusion. On this basis, we generate many ideas and beliefs that we take to be true. These ideas, foremost of which is the idea of being a fixed, permanent, and abiding self, then support and reinforce our illusion. It is very sad, really, that we are caught in a net of confusion with no obvious way out.

Seeing everything, including ourselves, through the lens of duality is the deep root of our sticky mind. It makes us rigid and inflexible. Thinking we are a separate self, we attach to our name, job, money, material possessions, pleasurable feelings, and so on. Our "I" produces strong, self-centered opinions and becomes more and more judgmental and competitive. We feel superior to others when we have more (pride) and inferior when we have less (jealousy). We categorize our experiences as either good or bad, pleasant or unpleasant. The people we know become either friends or enemies. Our dualistic mind fixes our reality into an extremely limited set of possibilities, and all our relationships, with ourselves and with others, become distorted. Living life far removed from our authentic, open nature makes us terribly unfulfilled and unhappy. No wonder we develop the habit of incessant complaining.

The Power of Seeing One's Own Faults

Buddhism stresses the importance of learning more about the five negative emotions and how they disturb our mind. At first, these five emotions might seem natural because we are so accustomed to experiencing and expressing them in daily life. But they are not natural, nor are they harmless. They are products of our sticky mind. Remember, sticky mind is emotion stuck in concept. The overriding concept that makes our mind sticky is the idea of being a solid "I." Whenever we reify the "I," we also reify the "other." This duality of subject and object, of self and other, invites all five poisons—anger, pride, jealousy, attachment, and ignorance—to come and make themselves at home. Then they seem normal to us. We don't recognize that they are wholly dysfunctional. And we suffer as a result.

When I say "suffering," I am referring to the Buddhist concept of *dukkha*, a Sanskrit word most often translated as "suffering." But something gets lost in this translation. A friend told me about a conversation she had with a young man whose girlfriend had just left him. They were discussing the Buddhist concept of suffering, and this fellow confidently proclaimed, "No, it is not true that suffering is part of our lives. I have never experienced suffering!" With curiosity, my friend pressed him to describe his experience of breaking up. He said, "Yes, I have heartache, stress, anxiety. Some days I cannot sleep from feeling depressed and angry. But I don't have suffering." Clearly, "suffering" is a word whose connotations are too narrow to convey what is meant here. For this reason, translators have also rendered *dukkha* as "pain," "unhappiness," "distress," or "dissatisfaction."

Dukkha is always expressed through the five emotions that disturb our mind and make us unhappy. When we are carried away by these five disturbing emotions, we lose touch with our fundamental goodness and experience dukkha. Therefore, indulging emotion does not work. Running away from or denying the existence of our emotions does not help either. Actively suppressing or avoiding our own experience is being blatantly dishonest with ourselves, and this also is not a solution. Fortunately, Buddhism teaches various ways to deal with our disturbing emotions. The basic idea is that, through care and love, we can come to know them and make friends with them.

Making friends with the five negative emotions is a process of healing and transformation. But any process of transformation initially involves some difficulty. We first must summon the courage to look at and face our faults. These faults are the emotional patterns that we fall into habitually and often unknowingly. When we don't recognize our habitual ways of thinking, feeling, and acting, we perpetuate the suffering they create for ourselves and others. Because of ego-clinging—the tendency to reify and glorify the self—it is very difficult for us to see, let alone admit to, our faults. Seeing our faults can bring us down, making us feel bad about ourselves. We fail to recognize the tremendous opportunity finally being honest with ourselves presents.

Seeing our own faults and being aware of our negative emotions requires treating them with tender kindness, without judgment or blame, and embracing them with understanding. Once we can do this, the rest is quite simple. It is about showing up for our emotions when they arise, like a real friend. Genuine friendship can only be developed when there is honesty and open sharing from the heart. Be a genuine friend to yourself and accept whatever emotions, thoughts, and sensations arise in your mind. And be there for them. Seeing your own faults and making friends with your emotions could be one of the most powerful choices you make because you are being fully present for yourself.

Detecting Your Sticky Mind

One problem we encounter when dealing with our negative emotions is that we too easily identify with them. Identifying with an emotion prevents us from adopting a stance from which we can see it and change it. Then we are especially stuck. When we are angry, we think we have an angry mind. When we are happy, we think we have a happy mind. But how many minds do we have? In actuality, we have only one mind.

The Buddha taught that ending suffering is more than symptom relief—we must eradicate suffering's root cause. The eighth-century Indian scholar-practitioner Shantideva illustrated this point with an analogy. He observed that if we want to walk through a thorny field, it is not practical to cover the entire area with leather so that we can cross the ground barefoot; it is much smarter to use a small amount of leather to cover our feet. Similarly, it is not practical to try to control every external factor that might evoke our afflictive emotions; it is much smarter to address the root cause, the sticky mind.

The emotions that disturb our mind vary in strength depending on the degree of our mind's stickiness. The stickiness of our mind can be as slight as a simple remembrance, like in the case of my remembering the incident with the dog owner in Jackson Hole. Or it can be as strong as an addiction or obsession. Most often, however, it is something in between. But regardless of its strength, it binds us.

We generally assume that we only attach to things that we like. Recent research shows that wanting does not necessarily equate to liking.[2] Consider an example: the habit of drinking coffee. Do people drink coffee because they like it and enjoy it? Perhaps this is the situation for many people, but for the coffee addict, wanting somehow becomes detached from liking. When a coffee addict sees a coffee machine, the person's brain might release the neurotransmitter known as dopamine, which brings a pleasant chemical reward. Although the person follows through and drinks the coffee, the person doesn't enjoy drinking it. This example from science accords with Buddhism's observation that attachment is not about the external objects of our clinging—be they our car, money, house, clothes, shoes, or coffee—it is about sticky mind. Sticky mind is the reason behind the clinging, the habit, the attachment. Because our mind is sticky, our wanting is endless.

A student was puzzled by this idea and said, "But if we don't have any attachments, we can't enjoy anything in life." He told me that when he looked at his mind, his attachments looked very positive and nice. The problem is that in attachment our simple desire grows into wanting or craving, and then craving (a mental state) develops into grasping (an action). To state it another way, we obsess over those things we desire and then act toward them compulsively. This pattern becomes an inflexible habit. As we get habituated to whatever pleasure the original object of desire might give us, we want more and more of that same feeling. Our craving and wanting grow immeasurably. The result is that we lose awareness and forget what kind of person we are. In the short term, attachment, as well as pride, anger, and jealousy, might be seen as advantageous or even necessary to survive in a competitive world. But in the long term, these emotions hinder our development as spiritual beings and deprive us of opportunities to change.

Being aware of our attachment and its underlying cause (sticky mind) does not mean that we should not enjoy our lives. For instance, I quite enjoy a special blend of Starbucks Caffè Latte: two shots of espresso with steamed milk mixed with a half-shot of hazelnut syrup, a pinch of nutmeg, and lots of cinnamon. So delicious. But when I don't have the Starbucks latte, I am still fine because my mind is not "stuck" on Starbucks coffee. The liking has not developed into a mental affliction and turned into the endless wanting associated with obsession or addiction. If you appreciate coffee like I do, does your enjoyment of coffee have a sticky quality to it? What about other objects of enjoyment? It is a good practice to reflect on our own sticky mind so that we can identify where we get stuck and start learning to let go.

Applying the Antidote

The first step in overcoming sticky mind is to acknowledge our negative emotions. The next step is to gain familiarity with these emotions and apply their antidotes. These antidotes involve summoning a particular positive emotion or attitude to replace the negative emotion. Just as darkness cannot coexist with sunlight, negative emotions cannot coexist with positive emotions. If we apply these antidotes with consistency and determination, eventually our negative emotions will cease and positive emotions become second nature.

The antidotes for our negative emotions are quite straightforward. When anger arises, apply loving-kindness. When pride is present, remember to be humble. It can help to reflect on other people's good qualities instead of your own. When jealousy creeps up, learn to rejoice in other people's achievements. Enjoy their success as much as you would enjoy your own. When attachment is present, try to practice giving with generosity. As for ignorance, gain awareness of your blind spots and learn to see clearly. For example, you might seek clues in how other people or situations reflect you back to yourself. Loving-kindness, humility, joyfulness, generosity, and clear seeing act as antidotes to the emotions that disturb our mind. Applying these antidotes is an effective way to free ourselves from our mind's stickiness and start opening to our true nature.

As mentioned earlier, our mind is sticky because we fixate on the self. When we stop fixating on the self, positive qualities naturally radiate. These positive qualities protect us and preserve our peace of mind. They are a conscious response based on awareness of our negative emotions and the resolve to be free of them. Check for yourself: When you are loving and kind, can your anger easily arise? Not really, right? When we start to dwell in our positive qualities, it is like the rising of the sun—darkness vanishes, and light automatically shines. Our whole environment brightens. We see clearly and feel happy.

But in our current state, our sticky mind reverses our quest for happiness, and we ourselves are always its victim. Our afflictive emotions are sticky mind in action; they do not reflect who we truly are, our inherent nature. They are habitual patterns we have learned, and therefore they can be unlearned. The key is to remember that sticky mind is at the root of our negative emotions and to apply the antidotes to transform them. In this way, eventually we can eliminate sticky mind altogether. The Buddha taught that when the veil of negative emotions is lifted, wisdom naturally appears. Each of the five poisons is a wisdom that has been distorted by the confusion of ego-clinging. Applying the antidotes enables us to free our wisdom from this confusion and let it shine.

Knowing that it is possible to weaken and eventually abandon habitual identification with our negative emotions may sound hopeful to you. Recognizing that this process creates an opening to our inherent wisdom and the cultivation of dignity may be especially inviting. But we cannot let this potential remain merely an intellectual idea. If we do, our minds will cling to this notion in the same way that they continue clinging to external objects. We must instead actualize this understanding and cultivate a new relationship with our emotions. We do this through meditation.

I began my training in meditation very early, and from a young age I have meditated every day without fail. Well, almost every day. After I completed my formal monastic studies, as is common in my tradition, I chose the path of a "householder" and got married. Many years ago, while on vacation in Virginia with my wife and our two children, I completely stopped my practice for seven days. I was curious to see what would happen. I didn't do any meditation sessions, and I didn't read any meditation books. I just did normal things like working out, eating bagels, watching movies, and going shopping. I checked some emails and did some light work. For two days, it was okay. By the third and fourth days, I felt a little bit light, like my mind was not grounded—it felt like I was floating. I became a little moody and reactive. By the fifth and sixth days, I didn't feel very patient or understanding. For example, one day my son entered the room to ask a question while I was watching a movie. Feeling disrupted, I raised my voice: "What do you want?" Immediately, I recognized the negative effect of letting my mind do whatever it wanted. Without the mental stability that comes from meditation practice, my attention almost involuntarily wandered from one moment to the next, from one shiny object to another. Because my mind was distracted, my negative emotions grew. I was not in my natural state.

If we can always maintain the true natural state of mind, emotions will appear and disappear like the passing clouds, leaving our mind undisturbed. But recognizing the natural state requires a wider, more open mind than our present stickiness allows. Therefore, we must first work directly with emotions to make sure that our mind is pliable, open, and receptive. When the coarse forms of sticky mind are weakened, we can then work to remove subtler forms.

DIGNITY TRAINING

Breathing to Restore Balance between Body and Mind

Breathing is so natural that we may wonder why we would need to train in it. When we have sticky mind—when emotion is stuck in concept—our body and mind are thrown out of balance. We can use our breathing process to restore the balance we have lost.

> To start, recall the basic principle introduced earlier.

> *Body on the cushion.*
> *Mind in the body.*
> *Mind at rest.*

> Sit in a comfortable position with your body relaxed and spine straight, eyes gently open, mouth slightly open. Breathe naturally.
> Although later we will be meditating on the breath's natural movement, for our current purposes, we want

to deliberately breathe in and breathe out fully through the nose. Here, "fully" means to inhale through the nose, into the lungs, all the way to the belly; then exhale so completely that your belly contracts, forcing the last remaining air out. This kind of breathing calms the mind down very fast. There is no need to do this for very long. Just a couple of minutes to begin would be good.

> If you notice emotions or thoughts arising, you can change the practice in the following way. Breathe in naturally and then exhale fully, holding for one or two seconds before inhaling again. This breathing exercise works especially well when you have too many thoughts or a lot of anxiety.

Tame an Emotion

A powerful way to transform our negative emotions is to notice them both during and after meditation. For the purposes of this exercise, sit in a contemplative state. Recall a situation in which you experienced one of the five afflictive emotions—anger, jealousy, pride, desire, or ignorance. As you mentally revisit the details of that experience, really feel the emotion coming up, but try not to get lost in it. See if you can notice the sticky mind hidden underneath. Does awareness of the emotion weaken its strength? Now you've started the process of gaining greater awareness of your emotional life.

Pick one of these emotions to work with for one week and commit to noticing that emotion whenever it arises. For example, if you choose anger, notice whenever a feeling of anger arises in your day-to-day activities, whether a mild sense of offense, a lingering resentment, or full-blown rage. Recall the antidote for the emotion you choose, in this case loving-kindness, and apply it on the spot. The following week you can choose a different emotion to work with.

Inspirational Support

> It is hard to see one's own faults.
> So pointing them out to oneself is a crucial instruction.
> In the end, when faults are, one by one, removed
> Enlightened qualities increase and shine forth.
>
> DUDJOM RINPOCHE[3]

Noticing, Not Judging

There is a Zen story about a man riding a horse that is
galloping very quickly. Another man, standing alongside
the road, yells at him, "Where are you going?" and the man
on the horse yells back, "I don't know. Ask the horse."

THICH NHAT HANH[1]

Many people think of judgment as a positive quality. Therefore, when I explain in public talks that judgment is a
problem, I am often asked: "How can we function in life without judgment?" My answer is, "Actually, we will function better
because we aren't carrying the extra baggage of emotion that
clouds our experience."

For most of us, judgment is a subconscious habit. We constantly judge without knowing it, and we fail to recognize that
our judgments produce emotions that are harmful to ourselves
and others. These emotions in turn keep us from recognizing the
judgment that produces them. We judge all the time. We often
think or say, "I like this," "I don't like that," "This is good," "This is
bad." If we are being introspective, we also discriminate between
a "good thought" and "bad thought." But this kind of judgment

drives every one of our negative thoughts, emotions, and actions. Therefore, it would be most unfortunate to never know or examine how judgment is directing our lives. Letting judgment dictate our lives is like riding a wild horse we cannot control.

To function in life, we need less judging and more noticing. Noticing is neutral awareness without the baggage of emotion; with noticing, we see calmly and clearly without distorting what we observe. Judging, on the other hand, is a spark that often ignites the fire of negative emotion and action. The fire of emotion obstructs our vision and distorts our perception, preventing us from seeing situations clearly. In this way, noticing and judging have opposite effects.

At the experiential level, the difference between noticing and judging can be subtle, but there is a simple way to distinguish between them: if when noticing or observing something emotions also arise, we are judging, not simply noticing. To put it simply:

Judging has a tail of emotion that noticing does not.

The tail of emotion that gets attached to noticing is extra baggage. We don't need it. Therefore, a crucial step in cultivating dignity is learning to notice whatever is happening in our experience without the contaminating influence of negative emotion. This includes noticing not only events in our environment but more importantly our own thoughts, emotions, and actions.

Here is a story a student, whom I will call Tim, shared with me about a time when his judgment ran like a wild horse, creating negative emotion and a strong reaction. Tim was driving home after a long day at work. He was quite exhausted, and as usual, the rush hour traffic was heavy. When he exited the highway and signaled to get into the far-right lane to turn, a car with tinted windows sped up and blocked him.

A thought instantly arose in his mind: "How rude! He knows I'm going to that lane but deliberately speeds up. Now I'm going to miss my turn!"

Tim felt additional frustration that the other driver's tinted windows prevented the satisfaction of communicating a nasty glare. Infuriated, Tim honked his horn forcefully. Only moments later did he realize he could turn right from the lane he was in. The practical reality was that the other driver's actions had not actually inconvenienced him.

When Tim told me this story, he said, with embarrassment and regret, that he lost his dignity that day by becoming momentarily enraged and reactive. Tim had been practicing meditation for years. He realized almost immediately after the incident that instead of remaining grounded in his good nature, he had let his self-centered, judging mind take over. Rather than simply noticing that the lane was blocked and calmly negotiating the situation, Tim's strong judgment became a wild horse directing his thought, emotion, and action. It took him somewhere he had not intended, somewhere he instantly regretted. Everything happened so quickly: judgment arose spontaneously and was immediately followed by the emotion of anger and the action of forcefully honking the horn. This is the hidden power of judgment to distort our perspective and lead us to act in dysfunctional and potentially harmful ways. We all have moments like this, moments when we are completely at the mercy of our negative emotions and the judgments that accompany them.

How often does a judgmental thought about a random person ruin your day? How easily and quickly do such thoughts solidify and stir up emotion? How suddenly do these emotions incite action?

When our mind is fragile, judgmental thoughts and attitudes can easily provoke such chain reactions, suddenly catapulting us into dramas, big and small. When this happens, we lose all contact with our inner dignity, which by sharp contrast has the quality of clarity and stability. What can we do to defuse the chain reaction of thought inflaming emotion, and emotion agitating into action? Of course, it would be ideal to tame our judgment right from the start, but in all practicality, it is easier to detect thought, emotion, and action than the judgment behind them. Therefore, a good place to start is simply noticing our thoughts.

Noticing Thoughts

Noticing a thought when it first arises is crucial for stopping the downward spiral into additional thoughts, emotions, and actions that could otherwise ensue. Our thoughts have the power to enslave us when we are not aware of how they function in our mind. But we can take command of the situation. How do we do that? It is simple.

Notice the thought as thought.
Let it be.
Do not judge.
Rest the mind.

Let me say a little bit more about this. We notice the thought at the very moment it forms, and we recognize that it is only a thought. As you become more familiar with thoughts, you will see experientially that they are not solid but rather ephemeral. They are merely thoughts. Next, we let the thought be, not manipulating it in any way. We especially don't judge the thought as good or bad. If we are successful, the thought will naturally dissolve, and then we rest the mind. In resting the mind without thought, we return to the state of clarity and stability that characterizes our inner dignity. As we become more familiar with this way of being, we will be able to detect our judging mind and tame it.

Thoughts only have power over us when we follow them and take them too seriously. Because of this, some people ask me, "How about stopping thoughts so that they don't create emotions that make us upset?" A friend told me that she saw a sign at a yoga studio, "Come to learn meditation and stop your thoughts." I was puzzled because this was new to me. I have to admit that in my meditation training, I have never learned to stop my thoughts. On the contrary, I was taught by my teachers that thoughts enter and leave our mind naturally, in a ceaseless flow. And even though we tend to attribute great importance to our thoughts, they are not solid and don't have intrinsic existence.

We must acknowledge that suppressing our thoughts would never work because thoughts are natural activities of the mind; they are endless and unstoppable. On the other hand, resigning ourselves to our thoughts would be disastrous because of how quickly and easily they can develop into afflictive emotions and unwholesome actions if left unchecked. The humorist Mark Twain is said to have quipped, "I have lived through some terrible things in my life, some of which actually happened." In other words, when we fail to recognize our thoughts as thoughts, we can live through all sorts of imaginary suffering.

When we recognize our thoughts as thoughts and don't judge them as good or bad, we can use them in a way that aligns with our inner dignity and promotes peace and happiness; otherwise, they shape us in ways that can alienate us from ourselves. As the Buddha put it:

> We are what we think.
> All that we are arises with our thoughts.
> With our thoughts we make the world . . .
> Your worst enemy cannot harm you
> As much as your own thoughts, unguarded.[2]

Buddhist masters use the analogy of a sprout and tree to talk about thoughts. When you plant a seed and it starts to sprout, you can easily cut it with your fingernail. After ten years, when the sprout has grown into a strong tree, you will need an ax to cut it.

A thought is like a young sprout—it is easy to uproot. But when a thought grows into an emotion and later an action, removing it requires the mental equivalent of an ax.

To gain freedom from enslavement to thoughts, we must learn to notice them and let them be without judging them. In this way, we neither follow thoughts nor suppress them. When we don't get caught up in thoughts, and we don't let them hang around unnoticed, we eventually see beyond them, glimpsing the inner spaciousness of our indestructible dignity. Until then, this inner spaciousness is something we rarely experience directly. It is always present beneath the surface though usually obscured by the frequent and persistent thoughts and emotions overcrowding our mind. When we let our thoughts be, they no longer distract us. They naturally calm down, and we start to see beyond them to gain contact with our true nature.

The process of noticing a thought as thought might be difficult for many people, especially at the beginning. Our mind has the habit of wandering away from awareness. One popular meditation technique for noticing thoughts is labeling them. No matter which thought arises while sitting in meditation—whether it is simply the image of a friend or thinking about what you will have for dinner—you mentally label your experience as "thinking." When you become more focused on a sound, such as the sound of a passing car, you think, "Hearing." The idea is to increase awareness of what is happening in your mind without getting caught up in the content of your thoughts. Labeling can help some people bring wandering thoughts back to awareness, but eventually it is good to move beyond the labeling technique and work with thoughts more directly.

Our thoughts are not us, and we are not our thoughts—even so, we commonly identify with them. Underneath the constantly arising, scattered thoughts, our mind is always present and clear, with the power to know and transform. This clear and knowing mind is who we truly are. The moment we identify with this dignified ground of being, we can recognize when our mind is at rest and not carried away by judgment. If we practice noticing without judging like this for a while, freedom and strength will grow within us. We then become mature adults able to see the comings and goings of thoughts as no more real than the games children play. We don't take them too seriously, and we definitely don't let them ruin our day.

A Technique for Taming Thoughts and Emotions

One of the root causes of suffering is having a thought instantly arise without recognizing it. Our lack of recognition gives this thought the power to grow into a tree of negative emotion and judgment without knowing what has happened until it is too late. If we become aware of our thoughts as they arise, the power of negative emotion and judgment will weaken. They may remain present in a subtle form, but they will be less apt to activate in full-blown ways that create disturbance.

The Buddha taught a very elegant, effective, and simple meditation technique for instantly weakening thoughts. This technique was promoted by an eleventh-century Indian meditation master and scholar named Atisha, who learned it from a famous teacher-scholar named Dharmakirti. I learned it from my teacher Nyoshul Khen Rinpoche. In Tibetan, this technique is named *purjom. Pur* means "arising," and *jom* means "to cut at once." Therefore, purjom means "to cut at once upon arising." In purjom meditation, the moment a thought arises, you look directly at it. When you are successful, the thought will immediately dissolve. That way, we cut the thought the moment it arises.

You might be wondering how to look directly at a thought. Obviously, we can't see thoughts with our eyes; we can only see thoughts with our mind, or what I've heard referred to as the "mind's eye." When we see a thought with our mind, we ordinarily only see its content. Grasping at a thought's content rapidly generates many further thoughts. We can reverse this pattern by bringing awareness to the thought itself. When you notice a thought without getting caught up in its content, it simply dissolves.

Let's use a thought laced with anger as an example. When you have an angry thought, do not ask why you are angry. Instead, just turn inward and look directly at the angry thought itself. When you look at it directly, the thought immediately dissolves and loses its power. If another thought comes up, repeat the same procedure: Look at the thought and watch it dissolve. No thought seen in this direct way will remain for a long time. This is called "using the mind to look at thought." When you look, you will see that the thought arises, and then the thought ceases. No thought remains permanently. Every second, thoughts come and go; they are not as solid as we think. Now we are gaining experience regarding something that would otherwise remain an intellectual idea.

If we look carefully, we will see that anger arises in three stages. These stages pertain to thought, emotion, and our physical body. In the first stage, we see an arising thought whose content is typically about having been slighted or having had a desire frustrated. In the second stage, this thought generates additional thoughts, weaving a narrative accompanied by the emotion of anger. Finally, in the third stage, a physical reaction occurs. From these angry thoughts and emotions, we experience the physical feeling of anger arising in our body.

Some people think it is okay to be angry so long as we don't act on it by screaming and shouting at other people. If no one is on the receiving end, they believe, no harm is done. I don't think this is an accurate understanding of anger. In my experience, anger is always an action; it acts like a verb and not a noun. Anger, in both its gross and subtle forms, actively blocks the door to wisdom and compassion. It commits an internal violence, even if not an external one.

Taming thoughts and emotions in this way is extremely important at the practical level. It prevents us from giving our control to a wild horse taking us places we don't want to go. But the purjom technique has another important function. By looking at our emerging thoughts and emotions and seeing them dissolve of their own accord, we catch a glimpse of their genuine nature. We generally tend to believe that thoughts and emotions are real things that truly exist. But when we examine them, they disappear. How can they be real? Therefore, in addition to helping us solve practical problems as they arise, purjom reveals to us the true nature of our mental reality. This kind of direct insight is deeply transformative.

Someone once commented to me, "You said that thoughts would naturally dissolve. Where do they go?" As I mentioned earlier, thoughts are like waves in an ocean. They come and go, ceaselessly. Waves do not go anywhere. There is nowhere for them to "go." They are part of the ocean and will remain part of the ocean. The ocean, unaltered by the waves, is our true nature and will remain unchanged by our thoughts, emotions, or judgments.

DIGNITY TRAINING

Looking Directly at Thoughts

> Begin by getting into meditation posture as describe previously.
> Use one of the breathing meditation exercises to calm your mind and cultivate some measure of mindful awareness.
> After you feel relaxed and focused, release your focus, and look at your mind.

> When you see a thought, simply look at it. Do not label it, and do not follow it, meaning do not get caught up in its content. If you are fully present to the thought itself, you will see it dissolve. This is the purjom technique described earlier.

> After the thought dissolves, you will experience an open awareness. Rest in that for as long as it remains.

> When a thought arises again, apply the same technique.

If you do not yet have much experience with meditation, you might find this exercise challenging. That is okay. You can simply continue developing mindfulness with the earlier exercises. Eventually, looking at thoughts and watching them dissolve will become easy.

Looking Directly at Emotions

When we apply the purjom technique to break the endless proliferation of thoughts, we also undercut any emotions that might have been generated and any negative actions that might have ensued. If we are unsuccessful in applying the first step of looking directly at a thought itself, then we can instead look directly at the emotion that arises from the thought. If this is successful, the emotion will dissolve immediately and not have the opportunity to express itself as an action in the world.

Inspirational Support

Instead of chasing the anger, just be gently aware. Don't reject it, but don't dwell on it either. Just turn your attention to look gently at the thought. At that moment of turning inward to just observe, the thought will dissolve. At that moment, just exhale and rest.

Then, after a moment or two, it will come back. So just turn to observe it again. It will dissolve. Keep practicing like that, and the power of the anger to ensnare you will be weakened. You won't be overpowered by the rawness of the emotion because you won't let it establish itself; you won't cling to it.

ORAL TEACHING OF
NYOSHUL KHEN RINPOCHE,
AS RECALLED BY
PHAKCHOK RINPOCHE

7

Healing from the Habit of Judgment

Changing habits is like straightening a tightly wound scrap of paper. You unfold the paper and straighten it out, but if you let go of it, it rolls right back up by itself.

ORAL TEACHING OF TULKU URGYEN RINPOCHE,
AS RECALLED BY PHAKCHOK RINPOCHE

I once was teaching a meditation retreat when I overheard a student complaining about another student. He spoke in a very animated, agitated way for some time. As the retreat went on, I recognized this had not been an isolated incident—on this retreat, several students were having conflicts and complaining among themselves. Conflict with other people is inevitable in life and can be dealt with skillfully, leading to resolution and a strengthening of bonds. But conflict that ends in complaining only creates additional trouble and becomes a perfect breeding ground for disharmony. I was sad to see this happening.

At the next day's teaching session, I made a point of distinguishing between complaining and sharing one's difficulties.

When we complain—in this instance, about another person—we speak out of agitation, which only serves to reinforce the conflict. By contrast, when we share our difficulties, we rely on the kindness of others to help us gain perspective on our conflict and helpful insight into how we can resolve it. It is okay to share difficulties with another person who willingly provides a sympathetic ear, but it is a problem to complain. Sharing difficulties helps us recognize and accept our responsibility and learn; complaining only serves to abandon responsibility and strengthen the habit of judgment.

What we repeatedly think, say, or do every day becomes habit. Oftentimes, habits are formed without our awareness. This is unfortunate because the deep-seated habitual patterns in our thoughts, words, and actions often cause tremendous difficulty for ourselves and for others. This is especially true of judgment. "Of all habits, the habit of judgment is the hardest to tame," my grandfather once reminded me.

Why is the habit of judgment so difficult to tame? It is because it is difficult to notice judgment. We usually are not aware of our judgment until we see its aftermath. By then we find ourselves entangled in a knot of thoughts, emotions, and actions that is impossible to untie. Gross expressions of judgment include holding strong opinions about oneself and others. Some expressions of judgment are so subtle as to escape detection altogether, such as grumpy little thoughts like "I don't like this" or "I don't like that." But regardless of how judgment expresses itself, its source remains a mystery to many of us. How did we become so judgmental?

Mapping Judgment on Our Arm

Because our judging mind is hard to see, we start with understanding our thoughts and emotions. But not all thoughts affect us the same way. What usually causes us trouble are our disturbing or negative thoughts.

As previously mentioned, the Buddha taught that we tend to be afflicted by "five poisons." Recall that these are the four emotions of anger, jealousy, pride, and attachment, in addition to the blind spot by which we are completely unaware of what is happening (also known as ignorance). Where do these five poisons come from? They come from judgment. If the five poisons come from judgment, where does judgment come from? It comes from our ego-clinging or self-cherishing.

We can understand these relationships better by analogy with the human body. In the same way that my teacher Nyoshul Khen Rinpoche used the five fingers as a metaphor for the five levels of motivation, I have found the five fingers to be an ideal way of describing how the negative emotions relate to judgment and ego-clinging. If the five poisons are our five fingers, judgment is like the arm, and ego-clinging is like the shoulder. Just as our five fingers connect with the arm by way of the hand, so too are the five poisons rooted in judgment. Just as the arm comes out of the shoulder, so too does judgment arise from our ego-clinging. Here's a simple illustration to make it clear.

| Five fingers | ← | arm | ← | shoulder |
| Five poisons | ← | judgment | ← | ego-clinging |

When we don't know this relationship between the five poisons, judgment, and ego-clinging, our mind is blind—we can't see clearly what is driving our actions. Therefore, to transform our mind, we must take care of judgment. As I discussed earlier, judgment can be understood as noticing with a tail of emotion added. This tail is often hidden from us. When we don't see the emotion that accompanies judgment, we erroneously think we are simply noticing.

So how can we see our judgments? We can see them through self-reflection. In the beginning, we may not notice our judgments at all. As we continue reflecting, the judgments we start noticing will be strong, fast, and reactive. This is gross-level judgment. As we continue reflecting, the judgments we notice become more and more subtle.

Our mind is beautiful, really. When we are completely sincere in examining our faults, simply recognizing a judgment instantly dissolves much of it. In an instant, we can take care of a big part of our judgment. But to be able to do this takes time and practice. It is not always easy to notice our own judgment. Fortunately, we can train ourselves to do so, and the reward is immense.

Love Is Freedom from Self-Judgment

The topic of self-love has become very popular in contemporary times. Traditional Buddhist teachings do not mention this concept, but the Buddha did give many teachings on loving-kindness and compassion. These attitudes don't focus on ourselves per se but rather our interconnectedness with all others and the altruistic intention to help them. For example, when practicing loving-kindness, we recite the wish, "May all beings have happiness and the cause of happiness." When practicing compassion, we think, "May all beings be free from suffering and the cause of suffering." Because people are often so focused on self-love, they want to be sure they are not left out. Therefore, I often hear the question, "Does 'all beings' include me too?" Of course, the answer is yes, but the focus is different. It may seem ironic, but our own happiness comes from focusing on the welfare of others, not ourselves. This is because when we focus on ourselves directly, we tend to fixate on ego. But when we focus our love on "all beings"—which includes us, though only indirectly—the benefit to us is much greater.

In our contemporary world, everything is accelerating, physically and emotionally. Our resources are taxed. Perhaps because it is impossible to meet all the demands placed on us, many people have developed some form of self-hatred and are searching for a cure. Many assume the cure for self-hatred is self-love. But what is this "self-love"? Why do people emphasize it so much?

I have been pondering these questions. What I've found is that the desire for self-love is really a cry to be free from self-hatred. And self-hatred arises when we judge ourselves. Therefore, the desire for self-love is really the desire to be free from the tyrannical judgments we hold toward ourselves. Have you ever experienced that after someone hurts your feelings for a few seconds, you end up hurting yourself over the course of many years? A word or a gesture by others may cause discomfort or even tremors within us. People in the grip of judgment are subject to wildly fluctuating extremes. When others agree with them, they feel like winners. When others disagree with them, they feel like losers. It is as if a tyrant lives inside them, constantly judging their every move.

This tendency toward judgment is a vulnerability, not a strength. No matter whether we are judging ourselves or others, we must ask "who" is judging. The "who" is "I." When there is a thought of "I," there is ego-clinging. Our ego wants to defend itself, so it judges others. When ego is not successful, it judges us. As a result, we become our own worst critic. Don't get caught up in this distorted game of separating "I" and "other."

Once you are free from self-judging, love spontaneously manifests. Because you are love, you don't need to proclaim it. Then, whenever you hear anything that anyone says about you, you won't react. You won't have the impulse to get revenge for their criticism of you, nor will you direct judgment toward yourself either. You may still feel hurt, but you won't be shaken to the core. Others cannot harm you. Similarly, if others praise you, you won't take it too seriously either and can avoid the temptation of self-inflation that leads to pride.

Anti-Judgment Medicine

As we have seen, our judging mind has a negative effect on both the judger and the judged. When we judge ourselves, this effect is all the greater. Therefore, in addition to reducing our tendency toward judgment through self-reflection and noticing, we must heal the wounds that our judging mind has inflicted on us. It's like looking at a poisonous snake bite: you know the snake has bitten you, but simply looking at the bite and knowing what kind of snake it was will not help at all. What you really need is the correct antivenom medicine.

In the case of judgment, this antivenom medicine is loving-kindness and compassion. Loving-kindness (*maitri* in Sanskrit; *metta* in Pali) is the intention and capacity to bring joy and happiness to oneself or other persons. Compassion (*karuna* in Sanskrit and Pali) is the intention and capacity to relieve the suffering of other persons or living beings.

Loving-kindness and compassion are qualities we can cultivate, and there are well-known meditations in the Buddhist tradition for cultivating each of them. Understand that these are not separate qualities. The loving-kindness practice generates both love and compassion, just as the compassion meditation cultivates both compassion and love. The dignity training at the end of this chapter combines them in a way that makes their effect more powerful.

The meditation on loving-kindness and compassion can heal old wounds and introduce a fresh perspective and attitude toward ourselves and others. As you will see shortly, the essence of this practice is to wish others happiness and freedom from suffering. At the beginning, this will be a mental exercise. You might not feel that your wish for others to be happy and free from suffering is genuine. That is all right. Little by little, bit by bit, your wish will become more sincere. Gradually, you will feel your heart opening. From knowing more deeply that, just like you, everyone wants to be happy and free of suffering, genuine feelings of compassion and loving-kindness will start to arise. You will feel humble, and your heart will become pure. You know your heart is pure when you can't identify anyone you dislike, hate, or have a grudge against.

The best way to bring about self-love, in effect, is by practicing loving-kindness and compassion meditation. When you let loving-kindness and compassion permeate your mind and heart, you no longer suffer from negative emotions and judgments. Due to the healing power of loving-kindness and compassion, you will be able to develop confidence in yourself and access your innate dignity.

DIGNITY TRAINING

Meditation on Loving-Kindness and Compassion

In this practice, rather than directly focusing on the breath as we did in chapter 5, we use the breath as an anchor while adopting a different focus for cultivating loving-kindness and compassion.

Find a quiet and serene place where you can do the following:

> Sit in a comfortable position and breathe naturally.
> If your mind is active, spend a little time focusing on breathing in and breathing out until the mind is peaceful and calm. Then proceed.
> Bring to mind someone who is suffering right now, be it be from pain, unhappiness, depression, or anxiety.

> As you inhale, wish this person to be free from suffering and the cause of suffering, mentally reciting: "Breathing in, I wish you freedom from suffering."

> When you exhale, make a deep wish for this person to have happiness and the cause of happiness: "Breathing out, I wish you happiness."

> Repeat these deep wishes, coordinating them with the natural cycle of your breath, while maintaining the mental image of the person whose suffering you want to relieve.

As you breathe in and out, you might want to use a hand gesture to strengthen your concentration. As you inhale, gently guide the palms of your hands toward your chest, stopping a few inches short of touching it. It is as if your hands are pulled in by the inhalation. As you exhale, gently flip your palms, and let them glide smoothly outward with your breath. Then flip them again and inhale. This technique is optional; use it if it is helpful.

Whether using your hands as a support or not, think of the person you are sending good wishes to and repeat these short phrases as many times as you can, letting the feeling of loving-kindness and compassion fill your heart:

Breathing in, I wish you freedom from suffering.
Breathing out, I wish you happiness.

If you cannot think of a specific person who is suffering now, you can begin this exercise with someone who is dear to you, such as a family member or a close friend. Then extend the same feelings to your friends' friends, then to strangers, people for whom you have neither affection nor animosity. Then extend these attitudes to "enemies," people with whom you are having or have had difficulties.

Eventually, we can extend these wishes to all beings: "I wish all beings freedom from suffering. I wish all beings happiness."

Inspirational Support

The practice of compassion begins at home. We have our parents, our children, and our brothers and sisters, who perhaps irritate us the most, and we begin our practice of loving-kindness and compassion with them. Then gradually we extend our compassion out into our greater community, our country, neighboring countries, the world, and finally to all sentient beings equally without exception. Extending compassion in this way makes it evident that it is not very easy to instantly have compassion for "all sentient beings." Theoretically it may be comfortable to have compassion for "all sentient beings," but through our practice we realize that "all sentient beings" is a collection of individuals. When we actually try to generate compassion for each and every individual, it becomes much more challenging. But if we cannot work with one individual, then how can we work with all sentient beings? Therefore, it is important for us to reflect more practically, to work with compassion for individuals and then extend that compassion further.

DZOGCHEN PONLOP RINPOCHE[1]

The Courage to Love

If you have a sincere and open heart, you
naturally feel self-worth and confidence,
and there is no need to be fearful of others.

THE FOURTEENTH DALAI LAMA[1]

The day was April 25, 2015, a Saturday. I was participating in an event at Shechen Monastery in Kathmandu, only a few minutes' walk from my house. Suddenly the earth shook, violently. As many objects in our surroundings crumbled, people attending the event started running out of the building in panic. My wife was also in attendance, and we immediately looked at each other. Our first thoughts, riddled with anxiety, were about our children, who were at home. "Are they safe?" we wondered. Luckily, they were. Even so, they were shaken by their first experience of the ground rumbling underneath them and objects falling in front of them. Later we learned that this was one of the deadliest earthquakes in Nepalese history. With a magnitude of 7.8, and followed by hundreds of aftershocks, it claimed almost 9,000 lives, left more than 20,000 people injured, and rendered hundreds of thousands of Nepalis homeless. Some villages were badly damaged or completely wiped out. It was devastating. The suffering this earthquake inflicted was unfathomable.

Yet, what happened next was remarkable. Because of my involvement with various monasteries in Nepal, I know many monks and nuns personally. Among them, there was little sign of trauma, despair, or overwhelming emotion, even though some originally came from villages that had been heavily damaged and where friends and family members had been lost. Instead of clinging to their personal losses and mournfully crying—"Why did the earthquake affect my friends and family?"—they remained calm and positive. Very quickly, several monasteries transformed into headquarters for disaster relief, and many of these monks and nuns immediately started helping to provide food, shelter, and medical supplies to those in need.

Helping to relieve the suffering of others and bring them happiness is the heart of the Buddha's teachings and therefore a regular practice of these monks and nuns. We human beings are far more interconnected and interdependent than we typically realize. I have found that in catastrophic natural disasters such as the Nepal earthquake, people become sharply aware of their interconnectedness and recognize that everyone, just like themselves, wants to be happy and not suffer. Whatever our personal circumstances with regard to financial status, gender, race, education, and so on, we all want to be safe, protected, peaceful, and happy. With this awareness, a spontaneous connection with others wells up inside us, and our hearts open. We want to help.

A Calm and Peaceful Mind

The earth continued to tremble. Grim predictions of major aftershocks kept us on our toes. There were bricks and debris as far as the eye could see. Meanwhile, most of us were crowded together in tents in open fields to avoid the danger of collapsing buildings.

Very soon, many people, not just the monks and nuns of the monastery, came to join the disaster relief effort. This included friends, friends of friends, neighbors, students of the monasteries, and complete strangers. They opened their hearts, prioritizing their desire to help others and alleviate suffering. Their bravery and courage in the face of natural disaster were extraordinary.

Buddhism has a term for those beings with the courage to love others fully, even in the face of the greatest challenges. We call them *bodhisattvas*. Bodhisattvas live by a pledge to put the welfare of others above their own. They recognize that the greatest happiness comes from benefiting others, and that self-absorption only brings misery. During the Nepal earthquake, these volunteers were acting like bodhisattvas, making a positive impact in the lives of others, and consequently benefiting themselves in the process.

The same loving qualities of a bodhisattva are always and already within us; they are the core of humankind and a touchstone of our inner dignity. Usually, these qualities lie dormant and seldom peek out, but catastrophe has a way of making them manifest in our spontaneous rush to assist others. My friends in America told me the same thing happened in 2001, immediately after the September 11 terrorist attacks on the World Trade Center and the Pentagon. People all over the country lined up at blood banks to donate blood for the injured victims in New York and Washington, DC. And we see similar instances all over the world. These events demonstrate that we all have these loving qualities inside us, and while the circumstances that occasion their rise to the surface are excruciating, it is heartening to see the fundamental humanity that emerges in full force as a result.

Most of us depend on external circumstances to bring forth our good qualities. For example, we may initially be eager to respond to the Nepal earthquake relief effort, but when the earthquake is over, so is our interest in helping. External conditions can be a powerful motivator for our good qualities to manifest, but when those same conditions cease to exist, we easily revert to the old pattern of caring primarily for ourselves. Our desire to help others withers away. Our good heart is such that we might sincerely intend to be kind and compassionate toward others, but the complex habits of our mind take us in the opposite direction. Our kindness and compassion ebb and flow, inconsistent and limited. Sometimes we are loving and kind and helpful to others. At other times we withdraw into ourselves and disconnect from others. We act in a self-centered way with little awareness of or concern for the consequences of our negative actions. We have a habit of disconnecting from our own best qualities!

Fortunately, we can change our habitual patterns and learn to be loving, kind, and helpful to others regardless of external circumstances. How do the bodhisattvas transform themselves so that their qualities of love, kindness, and compassion shine without obstruction?

Bodhisattva is a Sanskrit word that translates into Tibetan as *jangchup sempa*. It is telling to look more closely at the meaning of this Tibetan term. *Jangchup* points to a state of mind that has been purified of negative emotions, which is also a mind in which positive qualities have been permitted to blossom. *Sempa* means "bravery" or "courage." So, bodhisattvas are courageous beings who strive to benefit others purely out of compassion. The courage of bodhisattvas is grounded in a stable heart-mind free of negative emotions and infused with positive ones. This implies that developing the conscious and sincere intention to freely and generously help others requires that we free ourselves of our own disturbing emotions and cultivate a peaceful and calm mind. When we can maintain a calm and peaceful mind, our love and compassion become stable, strong, and ready for action. As we have seen, cultivating a clear and calm mind requires accurately seeing our current limitations, faults, and imperfections. We must first recognize and acknowledge the negative habitual tendencies that bind us before we can remove them to reveal the inner qualities of loving-kindness and compassion hiding underneath.

Softening the Heart with Understanding (Compassion)

If we look around with awareness and mindfulness, we can start to clearly see the kinds of suffering we discussed previously. Remember that suffering, or dukkha, doesn't necessarily mean torturing pain or overwhelming distress. It conveys a wide range of experiences involving discomfort, uncertainty, struggle, pain, or sorrow. Once we are born, we inevitably grow old, get sick, and die. And this is true of our loved ones as well. The suffering that comes from these experiences is unavoidable. Alongside more heightened difficulties such as wars, natural disasters, famines, and pandemics, we experience countless disappointments and emotional hurts throughout our daily lives. If we reflect with mindfulness, we can compose a surprisingly long list of experiences that are suffused with suffering. But don't just conceptualize this. Sit quietly, contemplating the reality of suffering, then put your hands on your heart. What do you feel about the suffering all around you?

We may start to feel the authentic desire to relieve or lessen the pain and sorrow of others, but despite having the best of intentions, we haven't yet developed the capacity to help in a truly effective way. If our compassion is emotional, remaining only at a feeling level, we may make things worse rather than better.

The cultivation of true compassion and loving-kindness requires wisdom. Wisdom transcends our ephemeral emotions and feelings, enabling us to see ourselves, others, and the world with clarity. Our negative emotions always distort what we see, whereas wisdom sees things as they truly are, unfiltered by our own issues, concerns, and reactivity. Wisdom and compassion work together as different yet related aspects of the same awakened heart. And wisdom plays an important role in softening that heart.

When we see others suffer, especially our loved ones, we naturally wish them to be free of their difficulties. But if we want to help them, we must learn to understand the factors that cause and support their suffering. Ordinarily, when we see a problem, we focus on the problem itself, not what is behind it. If we fail to address its root, the same situation will arise again and again. The solution is to cultivate and strengthen our ability to see and understand both the problem's underlying cause and its supporting conditions. The same principle applies whether we are talking about someone else's suffering or our own. The Buddhist tradition refers to these two factors by the familiar phrase "causes and conditions."

Simply put, "causes and conditions" means that nothing happens accidentally. Every appearance is a result of a multitude of interconnected causes and conditions. For example, when a tree bears fruit, the underlying cause of that fruit is the seed that originally germinated in the soil. The conditions that supported that seed developing into a tree include the soil, rain, sunshine, climate patterns, and many other factors too numerous to count. We can similarly reflect on and recognize the causes and conditions of our own suffering and that of others. Such understanding softens our heart. As this felt understanding becomes deeper and deeper, our heart opens wider and wider until it embraces every living being. Eventually, we come to understand that everyone, like ourselves, wants to be free from suffering and pain. We also understand what has led to that pain and what needs to be done to overcome it.

What are the causes and conditions that have produced the fruit of our suffering? We really should reflect on this. In the end, it comes down to not knowing ourselves, not knowing that our nature is pure. We don't realize that we are inherently loving, compassionate, and wise. Not knowing our true self leads to a tangle of negative emotions. This is the basic confusion at the root of our suffering. As with the fruit tree, the conditioning factors that support our suffering are countless. As we come to understand our own suffering, we come to understand the suffering of others.

True compassion arises with the understanding that other people are not their problems. Like us, their nature is pure, but they have lost sight of that. They have lost contact with their inner dignity. When we don't have that understanding for ourselves, when our own heart is narrow and rigid rather than open and soft, we tend to blame others for the mistakes they make. We fail to see all the factors contributing to their actions, thinking there is something fundamentally wrong with them. This then creates barriers to softening our hearts, instead of being compassionate and loving.

When we encounter difficult people who are suffering, it might not be easy to practice compassion correctly. Our heart may tense up and become rigid. When we see the mistakes they make, it is easy to quickly blame them for their misery, misfortune, and hardship, isn't it? But do we know the fabric of their days or the entirety of their life stories? Do we know what happens behind the scenes? Can we look beneath their façade to see the insecurity and confusion that lies within? Can we see the complex causes and conditions that have evolved into their misery, misfortune, and hardship?

Suppose you're standing in line to buy tickets for a movie. A woman comes from behind, bumps into you, and then scurries into the theater ahead of you. Your first thought might be something like "What a rude person! Who does she think she is to go in ahead of the rest of us waiting in line?" After you discover that her daughter was in the theater having a seizure, your blame and judgment disappear, and your heart softens. All that changed is your understanding. This is a simple example, but the same applies no matter the situation or the complexity of the factors involved. Compassion is always the appropriate response.

The blaming tendency springs from interpreting others through a narrow point of view uninformed by wisdom or understanding. When we are self-centered, we believe people deserve to be punished because of their wrongdoing. In Buddhism, there is no such concept as punishment. When we plant a fruit tree, we will get fruit. Similarly, when we make mistakes, we will get the result of our mistakes. It is not a punishment by anyone else or even from ourselves. It is natural law. If we can refrain from blaming others, we can soften our heart to see the causes and conditions behind their mistakes; our compassion and loving-kindness will grow and become vast and unbiased, like the sun shining equally on everyone.

Some people resist practicing compassion, thinking it will make them weak. They think their heart will become too soft. "Isn't it a weakness to be nice all the time?" a student once asked. I gave this question a lot of thought. "True compassion is not a sign of weakness," I told him. Instead, it is a sign of strength. Granted, if we only have emotional compassion, then our mind will be unstable, and that will make us weak. In this sense the student is correct, but only if we don't understand what compassion really means.

Emotional compassion is not all bad; it is a good starting point for compassion practice. But without wisdom, emotional compassion can lapse into the "blame game." As our compassion evolves to incorporate an understanding of causes and conditions, blaming stops altogether. We develop unconditional love for others and tremendous trust and confidence in ourselves. We find our inner dignity and learn to embrace it. When we combine dignity with compassion, we can see ourselves and others with clarity, and we feel the strong wish for others to be free not only from their immediate suffering but, more important, from the causes of suffering.

As to the student's fear that practicing compassion would make his heart too soft, that is not possible. The heart is already soft. When we speak of softening the heart, in a way this means softening the defenses that protect the heart from feelings of vulnerability. These defenses include our personality and character structure. We may say that we're tough, that we don't cry, or that we're not going to get all emotional and mushy. But no matter how hardened we might pretend to be, we all have the same soft, tender heart at the core of our being. What makes us truly tough is allowing ourselves to be vulnerable, lowering our defenses so that our heart can be touched. In this sense, compassion requires tremendous courage. At the same time, it requires wisdom so that when our tender heart is touched, we can still function.

The Love in Loving-Kindness
(Loving-Kindness)

The same is true with loving-kindness—it requires tremendous courage. Remember that in the Buddhist tradition, loving-kindness is the wish for all sentient beings to have happiness and the cause of happiness. No one would object to such a kind wish, right? Loving-kindness is one of the simplest, most natural, beautiful, and precious qualities of humankind. We all have experienced it, naturally. And yet, so often we think of love as something we give to others with the expectation of getting love in return.

As with compassion, a feeling of loving-kindness is not enough—it requires understanding. Without understanding there is no loving-kindness. What must we understand? We first must recognize that all living beings, humans and animals alike, are just like us in one essential way: we all want to be happy and peaceful.

Just as there are causes and conditions for suffering, there are causes and conditions for happiness. And love is wanting those causes and conditions for everyone.

At the beginning, our loving-kindness is like the shoot of a young plant that is vulnerable to external conditions such as wind or storms. It is partial in that we love ourselves and those close to us more than we love strangers, a bias arising from our habit of cherishing ourselves more than others. Through loving-kindness practice, our attitude toward others can change and expand to include larger circles of beings. The more we cultivate loving-kindness, the more we let go of our attitude of self-cherishing and the negative emotions associated with it, such as anger, pride, and jealousy.

When you radiate love, you naturally cannot be angry or look down pridefully on others. Instead, you see everyone and everything equally and clearly with the loving understanding that all appearances arise from a web of interwoven causes and conditions. Your loving-kindness becomes complete acceptance, without discrimination. Practicing loving-kindness like this obviously benefits others, but it especially benefits you. We all want love, but we usually think we need to find it from outside. In this case, rather than seeking someone else's love, you are love.

As you can see, in the Buddhist tradition, the practice of compassion and loving-kindness focuses primarily on others, not ourselves. There are good reasons for this. Our habitual self-cherishing tends to thwart our inner potential to be open, kind, and helpful. When we center our attention solely on ourselves, our heart-mind becomes narrow, mistakenly believing that we are isolated, independent, and solid. We forget that we are interconnected with other people, animals, the environment, and our communities. To have compassion and loving-kindness is to recognize and strengthen our connection with other living beings.

This can happen only when our heart is soft and open, not when it is rigid and inflexible.

Compassion and Love in Action

Recently, a student shared with me how illness softened his heart to others' suffering. Many years ago, he got sick with what seemed to be an unusual cold, but rather than getting better, he got worse. Eventually a specialist diagnosed him as having what is called chronic fatigue and immune dysfunction syndrome, an illness that can be as debilitating as it is mysterious. In the early months of the illness, he had to quit working. He decided to volunteer his time for an organization called Meals on Wheels, delivering food to the disabled and homebound.

At the end of his first day of delivering food, the student found himself filled with an inexpressible and unexpected joy. Feelings of warmth and tenderness, along with a profound sense of interconnectedness, rose in his heart. He felt happy that he had made a difference, no matter how small, in the lives of these individuals. This experience helped put his own illness into perspective. Seeing the suffering of others softened his heart, and compassion started to awaken. He felt so much more gratification from giving to those in need than he had ever felt from material possessions, mindless entertainment, or the praise of others.

A few years later, he gained full recovery from his illness. In time, he regarded his illness as a gift for the way it had shifted his life perspective. And he credited the softening of his heart through volunteer work as an important contributing factor to his recovery. Helping others in need had helped him face his own life in a new light. He learned that by benefiting others, he simultaneously benefited himself. Although he didn't think of it in these terms at the time, he was learning to selflessly wish others to be happy and free from suffering, and this brought a tremendous sense of fulfillment.

This student later became a professor at a university. One semester he randomly asked his students, "How many of you have ever done volunteer work?" He was pleasantly surprised when everyone raised a hand. He then asked, "How many of you found something unusually fulfilling in that work, something that no other experience could match?" To his astonishment, every person again raised a hand. His experience had not been unique. The desire to help others reflects something important in the human condition. He has repeated this experiment at different times with different groups of students, always with the same result. Within the hearts of these young students, and in all of us, there is sympathetic concern for the well-being of others. This good heartedness is a springboard for cultivating limitless compassion and loving-kindness. We can soften our hearts a little bit at a time, embrace people with love a little bit at a time, and strengthen our ability to be kind and helpful a little bit at a time. Step by step, we expand our capacity to cultivate a state of mind that can bring about the causes of compassion and loving-kindness in other people's lives. Then we will see that our compassion and love are ultimately limitless and boundless.

The Joy in Rejoicing (Sympathetic Joy)

Another way of expanding our capacity to love is by rejoicing in other people's happiness, success, and good fortune. But rejoicing for others is surprisingly difficult. Many of us find it easier to generate compassion for another person's sorrow than to feel joy in their success.

Imagine that one of our colleagues is receiving a promotion at work. Are we delighted in this person's happiness, or are we jealous? Perhaps we're thinking, "That promotion should have gone to me!" If so, we're creating suffering for ourselves, inevitably. When we have jealousy—a feeling of bitterness toward others who have something that we don't have—our mind becomes clouded. It becomes difficult to see situations clearly, and therefore to accept things as they are. When this happens, it is almost impossible to feel good for others. But we can reverse this tendency by simply taking delight in the happiness of others. Taking delight in the happiness of others immediately banishes our jealousy toward them while bringing up joy in ourselves. A simple example will make this clear.

A student and a few of her coworkers once were invited to the boss's house for a holiday party. The invitation card carefully listed every single coworker's most notable professional or personal achievement, such as reaching a sales quota, receiving an award, moving into a new house, or having a baby. This student's name was the only one not mentioned, even though she was invited. She wondered, edgily, "Why didn't my boss mention me?" She speculated that her boss had something against her or that she must not be good enough at her job. Then she worried about how others might perceive her. "My coworkers are probably laughing at me behind my back," she thought. Agonizing with all the doubts her mind had generated, she dreaded the party and couldn't bring herself to attend.

Later, when she learned about the practice of rejoicing in other people's achievements, the student was blown away. "It's so easy. I get it. It's like a light bulb suddenly being switched on," she remarked in earnest. Recounting the party incident in her mind, she watched as her overreaction quickly dissipated. For the first time, she could feel the joy in her coworkers' successes and achievements.

Rejoicing is often highlighted as an antidote to jealousy. But rejoicing is much more powerful than that because it can banish any negative emotion. In this student's case, it wasn't that she was jealous of others. Her habit of only focusing on herself and not seeing others had given rise to feelings of inadequacy and uncertainty. Rejoicing frees us from clinging to ourselves and helps diminish our sense of loneliness and isolation. We cannot have joy alone. Joy arises in us only when we recognize our connections with other people and appreciate their happiness and goodness.

Precious, Not Special (Equanimity)

In working with the volunteer team after the Nepal earthquake, I learned that the happiest volunteers were those who helped without discrimination or judgment. They did not exhibit any kind of hero or savior mentality, thinking they were special or better than others. By not discriminating between self and others, they offered their time and energy with peace and contentment. Because of their equanimity, they didn't take things personally, nor did they cling to either positive or negative experiences. This ability to see everyone as equal and to be content with whatever is happening is the foundation from which we can free ourselves of the negative tendencies of attachment and aversion.

Understandably, initially it might not be easy for many of us to have equanimity toward everyone. It's much easier to help people we like than those we don't. We must remind ourselves, however, that "like" and "dislike" are judgments. We've seen how destructive judgment is. Judgment reflects a mind stuck in emotion. It makes us biased and unable to see others clearly. If we can't see others clearly, we will be very limited in our capacity to develop compassion, loving-kindness, and joy. But when we cultivate equanimity, seeing all beings as equal and experiencing them that way, we eliminate judgment altogether. Then our compassion, loving-kindness, and joy have no limit. They can extend to all beings without discrimination. In this way, equanimity serves as a vital support to these other precious qualities.

A friend from Sweden once mentioned that part of Scandinavian culture is to not privilege oneself as special. "Don't think you are anything special" is number one in the ten rules known as "the law of Jante." The idea is described in a fictional story, but I was told that it is an unspoken social code throughout Scandinavia. Even though not included in formal education, this idea is ingrained in people from a young age. This notion of not cherishing oneself over others resonates with the Buddha's teaching on equanimity. The more we see that everyone is equal in wanting to be happy and free from pain, the more we, as a collective, can live in peace and harmony. Not putting ourselves above others—not feeling special—does not mean that we put ourselves down or feel indifferent. On the contrary, when we develop the quality of equanimity and see everyone as equal, we come to appreciate the precious existence of all living beings.

Equanimity is a state of mind free from anxiety, worry, and stress. When we have excessive worry or fear, it's hard to open our hearts to express love. Our worry and stress prevent us from seeing other people's worry and stress. When we are free of worry, not only can we see ourselves clearly, but we can recognize others' states of mind and relate to them with compassion and understanding. The differences between self and other, between friend and enemy, will naturally vanish.

Four Immeasurable Qualities of Love

Recall that bodhicitta, "the awakened heart," is the sincere wish to bring all beings to a state of perfect enlightenment and freedom from suffering. The essence of bodhicitta is to cultivate love motivated by this wish. Cultivating love this immense requires time, courage, and commitment. Through a gradual process, we develop all four qualities of mind described earlier: loving-kindness, compassion, joy, and equanimity. These four qualities are commonly known as the "four immeasurables." They are "immeasurable" because unlike ordinary feelings and emotions that come and go, their vastness knows no boundaries. When we practice cultivating these four qualities, our capacity to love expands so far and wide as to encompass the entire world and all beings in it. They are truly the abodes of true love.

It would be a mistake to think of these four qualities as separate from one another—the four immeasurables are fundamentally and thoroughly interconnected. For instance, when we train in loving-kindness, we wish for all beings to have happiness and the cause of happiness. By feeling this wish sincerely, we expand outward into the experience of those around us. As our tightness loosens, we feel the joys and sufferings of others more deeply, and we are moved to help them. In this way, our compassion grows. In addition, by wishing others happiness, we naturally take delight in their successes, increasing our sympathetic joy. As we become rooted in the purity of our intention, we cultivate an equanimity in which our distance from or closeness to others is no longer relevant to our wish that they be happy.

In these ways, these four qualities—loving-kindness, compassion, sympathetic joy, and equanimity—expand our capacity to love. This is the reason why the Buddha said they make us unshakable like a mountain. When our love is unshakable like a mountain, it is pure and without calculation. Our heart is warm, kind, and loving. It is tender and open to the suffering of others, never casting judgment or blame. We radiate joy as we celebrate others' happiness, success, and good fortune. And all the while, being deeply rooted in equanimity puts us completely at ease.

We've already seen an example of these qualities in action. Most Nepalis are not wealthy, but when the earthquake happened, so many of them came out to help the victims. Most remarkable was that they didn't ask for acknowledgment. This shows us that by not holding on to the feeling of being special or heroic, we can transcend personal fears and desires. Without calculating personal gain or loss, we can, simply and sincerely, express our natural positive qualities of love. Sometimes it takes particular circumstances such as a natural disaster for these qualities to manifest, but fortunately we can cultivate our bodhicitta so that we have access to these qualities all the time.

How do we cultivate bodhicitta? By making aspirations, which are mentally generated heartfelt wishes for the well-being of others. You might wonder how aspirations can help. This was the case for a kind-hearted friend, an environmental activist, who doubted this practice. "I can see concrete results from action, but I can't see what good wishing does," he told me. It might seem this way if we discount the role the mind plays in our lives. But as we know, the mind is of vital importance to everything we think, say, and do.

Traditionally, bodhicitta has two equally important aspects, known as "aspiration bodhicitta" and "application bodhicitta." We cannot have one without the other. Without making aspirations, the meaning of our lives is blurry. We don't know why we do what we do; as a result, our actions are not so effective. When we cultivate aspiration bodhicitta, our heart becomes sincere and unpretentious. We truly and deeply wish for all beings, without exception, to be freed of suffering and endowed with happiness. Such vast aspiration is the necessary ground for developing application bodhicitta; at that point, we can move beyond wishing for to acting toward the genuine benefit of others. In other words, it is only through aspiration that we can genuinely resolve to actualize our bodhicitta through action. This is the good that wishing does. Please don't underestimate its importance.

DIGNITY TRAINING

Meditation on the Four Immeasurable Qualities of Love
Foundational for cultivating bodhicitta (our awakened heart) is practice on the four boundless qualities of loving-kindness,

compassion, sympathetic joy, and equanimity (known as the four immeasurables). To bear fruit, these qualities must be cultivated repeatedly with sincere and keen enthusiasm.

> Begin by sitting comfortably in meditation posture.
> Take a few moments to connect with your breath and calm your mind.
> Now start contemplating how all beings are interconnected. We all depend on others just as others depend on us.
> Next, consider how much you want to be happy and to not suffer. Recognize that, in the same way, everyone wants to be happy and to not suffer.

Now we practice the four immeasurables. Although each immeasurable is presented one after another, you may prefer to focus on only one per session. Mentally recite the aspirational phrase provided below and spend some time contemplating the associated quality. See if you can connect your aspiration to a feeling of warmth in your heart, but if not, don't worry.

> Loving-kindness: "May all beings enjoy happiness and the causes of happiness."
> Compassion: "May all beings be free from suffering and the causes of suffering." To motivate this aspiration, you also can contemplate the measureless suffering that all living beings must endure, including all kinds of mental and physical struggles, illnesses, and pain. Contemplate not only the suffering itself, but the causes of suffering, foremost of which is not knowing our genuine nature.

> Sympathetic joy: "May all beings never be separated from the sacred happiness devoid of suffering." Really feel joy at the good fortune of others.
> Equanimity: "May all beings dwell in boundless equanimity that is free from attachment and aversion."

You can practice the four immeasurables before or after your formal sitting meditation. At the end of the session, rejoice in your effort and dedicate all the good your practice has generated to the benefit of all beings, sincerely wishing that it brings them to perfect happiness and complete freedom from suffering.

Practicing in this way will gradually remove our tendency toward self-cherishing and the dualistic distinction between self and other that underlies it. In other words, it will remove the obscurations blocking our inner potential to be fully loving and kind. With a heart truly awakened, we will then have the wisdom and power to benefit others as well as ourselves.

Inspirational Support

In your loving-kindness and compassion that is extended to all beings, there may be a subtle level of unconsciously thinking about how to benefit yourself. By continuously practicing that wish over time, selfishness is brought to the surface and exhausted through the power of the training. The wish becomes more authentic and genuine, as loving-kindness, compassion, sympathetic joy become very real and instinctive.

DZIGAR KONGTRUL RINPOCHE[2]

9

"Who Am I?"

Beings think "I" at first, and cling to self;
They think of "mine" and are attached to things.
They thus turn helplessly as buckets on a waterwheel,
And to compassion for such beings I bow down!

CHANDRAKIRTI[1]

"Who am I?" At first glance, the answer to this question might seem obvious. In my case, "I am Phakchok Rinpoche." But am I defined solely by my name? I am also the roles I adopt in my social relations—I am a son, brother, nephew, husband, father, teacher, student, author, monastery abbot, and so forth. Those are all true and valid. But is that all of who I am? Who am I as a person? What am I? My body? My consciousness? Something else? As we follow this question of who I am to look more and more deeply, it becomes quite complex! Or very simple, depending on how we look at it.

I was born into an illustrious Buddhist family. Tulku Urgyen Rinpoche, my famous grandfather whom you met previously, had among his children four sons who are prominent reincarnate lamas in the Tibetan Buddhist tradition, one of whom is my father. If I were to identify myself solely in relationship to my family, I might find myself having a difficult time. When we know ourselves solely through our relational social labels, we almost can't help but compare ourselves with others. Then we gauge our self-worth based on that comparison, which invites us to fall into a sea of negative emotions. It is easy to see that leaving our identity invested wholly in social relations can leave us with no end of misery and unhappiness. This way of thinking about who we are undercuts any hope of cultivating genuine dignity.

What is the solution? We must look more deeply at who (or what) we really are. Of course, I am a grandson, a son, and a nephew to my family. But this is only one aspect of who I am. We can always delve more deeply into what we identify as the self, beyond social labels and relationships. We can also look more deeply into our experience of being a self. These investigations are of vital importance in discovering the basis upon which we can cultivate dignity. Otherwise, if we stay at a more surface level, we will find our less deeply rooted understanding of self to be easily blown around by the winds of external circumstance, or as Chandrakirti puts it in the above quotation, we will "turn helplessly as buckets on a waterwheel." We must look beneath the surface of "who I am" to see ourselves and our situation in a realistic light.

Who Am I, Really?

Asking "who am I?" is surprisingly common. Whether explicitly or implicitly, many of us have asked this nagging question. And even if we haven't, our culture has. The theme of questioning personal identity is prevalent in philosophy, literature, and film. Consider Hamlet, the protagonist in Shakespeare's tragedy of the same name. He asks the equivalent of "who am I?" on multiple occasions and usually during a crisis, such as when his father dies, when his mother remarries, and when he is denied the throne.

Even popular movie characters such as Batman and James Bond have engaged in this kind of self-reflection. These fictional characters, like many of us, ask this question in times of crisis or in the face of impending death. When dire circumstances challenge our previous assumptions about who we are, we instinctively search for something beneath the surface of our usual identity, something to give us a deep and lasting sense of meaning and stability. Perhaps that instinctive search comes from the very thing we seek—our authentic nature.

But we don't have to wait for dire circumstances to ask this question. The Buddha encouraged his disciples to take a close look at the self (*atman* in Sanskrit; *dak* in Tibetan) before crisis occurs. We ordinarily think of the self as something that is singular, independent, and permanent. The purpose of this exploration is to question these assumptions through internal dialogue and appeal to ever deepening levels of our own lived experience. If we do have a solid, independent, and abiding self, we should be able to locate it logically and experientially, right? If we fail, then perhaps we need to rethink our assumptions.

The Buddha's interest in the question of self is not for the sake of intellectual or philosophical abstraction. This question is important because it is closely related to why we are happy or unhappy. Attachment to a misguided belief in an enduring self, the Buddha taught, brings us suffering. Conversely, nonattachment to the idea of a solid self contributes to our happiness.

When my teacher Nyoshul Khen Rinpoche introduced me to the question "who am I?" in my formative years, it opened the door for me to examine who I really am. That process challenged me to go beyond the social labels that had largely defined me to that point. It was a huge moment! It challenged everything I thought I knew about myself, and it greatly expanded my world.

Buddhism uses a concept called the "five aggregates" (*skandhas* in Sanskrit) to aid in that examination. The five aggregates are categories that summarize everything we could possibly experience. These aggregates are typically named (1) form, (2) feeling, (3) perception, (4) mental formations, and (5) consciousness. The first aggregate, form, refers to experiences that we would characterize as physical. The other four—feeling, perception, mental formations, and consciousness—are different aspects of mental experience. When we examine the aggregates, we come to realize our sense of being an individual "I" is just a concept that we affix to these interrelated and dynamic experiences. When we examine our experience in depth, we can't find an inherent self because the aggregates themselves are merely passing events. There is nothing solid or permanent about them, and therefore there is nothing solid or permanent about what we take to be our self.

Of course, this doesn't stop us from thinking of the aggregates collectively as "I" or relating to each of them as "mine." For example, we think that this is my body (form), my feelings, my perceptions, and so forth. "I" becomes the lens through which we view all experience. From society's point of view, being an "I" is legitimate and necessary. At the level of conventional reality, we need social identities to communicate with one another. So using "I" as a label is not a problem. Even the Buddha referred to himself as "I." What becomes problematic is when we cling to the idea that what the label points to is something permanent, abiding, intrinsic, and independent. This is called "ego-clinging." By thinking we can stand on something that in actuality is always shifting and groundless, we always feel a little shaky. To compensate, we express even greater confidence in who we think we are. Our ego becomes the center of our existence, and we attempt to protect it by being judgmental and competitive, while often underneath feeling fearful and needy.

In this way, ego-clinging fuels suffering. It suppresses and obscures our buddha-nature, which prevents us from contacting and expressing our inner dignity. Our conventional tendency of identifying "I" with our name, body, and mind unwittingly furthers ego-clinging and engenders dissatisfaction and confusion. Learning dignity is the process of gaining familiarity with our inherent nature, thereby freeing ourselves from the confusion of mistaken identity. Of course, we still use our social identity—for example, I am still Phakchok Rinpoche—but we don't lose ourselves in it.

There are three common misidentifications related with ego-clinging—thinking we are our name, thinking we are our body, and thinking we are our mind. Let's look at each of these beliefs in a little more detail, one by one.

Am I My Name?

The first question is "Am I my name?" Imagine someone asking you, "Who are you?" How would you respond? In most cases you would tell this person your name, right? But what's in a name?

Names are given to us after we are born, usually by our parents. Sometimes our name changes. In my case, I had a birth name, and later my tradition decided I would be "Phakchok Rinpoche." In other cases, a person may prefer a different name and even change it on their legal documents. This only shows that the name we identify with is in no way intrinsic to who we are. It could just as well be something else. Our surname does indicate our family, but that doesn't say anything about who we really are, about our fundamental nature. Yet we hold on to our name and take ownership of everything related to it, almost automatically, without careful scrutiny. When we have a prestigious title or rank added to our name, such as CEO or MD, we become even more invested in those labels. But if you are a CEO of a company, once you cease to be a CEO, are you still you?

As we can see, a name is a label used for the sake of convenience. Let's take this a little further. When we name something, we tend to think we are naming something substantial and lasting. When I was young, I was quite fond of cars. But what is a car? We know that a car consists of an engine, wheels, brakes, seats, and so on. We know a car needs gasoline or electricity to function. But is there a substantial, solid, unchanging, permanent entity called "car"? From the Buddhist perspective, a car is merely an assemblage of parts; there is nothing substantial to be found in what we call "car."

We can apply this analysis not only to our own name but also to what we call the "self." "Self" is a term we apply to an assemblage of different parts. We can name these different parts the "five aggregates." The self can only be said to exist in dependence upon these aggregates, and as we have seen, these aggregates themselves do not have inherent existence. Therefore, the self ultimately does not exist as its own intrinsic entity.

Am I My Body?

The next question is "Am I my body?" I have heard of something in the west called the "mind-body problem." This problem arises out of the belief that the body and mind are separate. This belief leads to confusion, and the language we use reflects this confusion. For example, when we say, "You bumped into me," we imply that we are our body. On the other hand, when we say, "You stepped on my foot," we seem to think we are the owner of our body. Am I my body, or am I something else that has a body? Isn't this confusing?

In the Buddhist tradition, we think the body has different levels: gross, inner, and secret. At the gross level, the body is the physical body. But the physical body—body in the gross form— is not separate from our mind. It is highly interrelated and interconnected with mind. We can see this with our analysis of the five aggregates. The form aggregate, or our experience of the physical body, clearly interrelates with our four mental aggregates. As a simple example, when we have a headache, we don't just experience our physical head. We also experience a feeling of aversion to pain, and we probably have lots of thoughts such as "I feel so miserable." In fact, if we feel aversion and reinforce it with our thinking, our headache almost certainly will feel worse! Just as our bodily experience impacts our mental experience, our mental experience impacts our bodily experience. We can see that even at the gross level, body and mind clearly are not distinctly separate.

Going beyond the gross outer body, the Buddhist tradition identifies an inner level called the "subtle body." The subtle body consists primarily of channels and winds. These channels and winds do not correspond to the physiological structures and functions identified in Western biology. Yet this subtle body is the place from which emotions emerge, and these emotions have a great effect on the physical body.

Beyond the inner level is an even deeper body called the "secret body." This "body" is our buddha-nature. It is referred to as "secret" because even though it is always there, we usually don't recognize it. In fact, many of us have no clue it is there to begin with. But it is a good thing it is there, because our buddha-nature, this secret body, is the deep source of our inner dignity and other genuine positive qualities.

As you can see, the body is much deeper than what appears to our physical senses. No wonder the body and its relationship to mind seem so mysterious. Buddhist philosophy considers the body not only important and powerful but also sacred. In fact, it is said that one hundred buddhas dwell in our body. This may sound mysterious, but it shows that in its depths our body is full of wisdom and compassion. But our body is also a reflection of the mind. When people have emotional unhappiness, this unhappiness often manifests in ways that harm the body. Still, we hold on to the physical body so strongly that we believe this is who or what we are.

Let's think about that. If I am my physical body, am I the skinny me in my youth or the chubby me that I am now? Am I my face, feet, chest, heart, hands, or fingers? Is there one place in my body that is "I"?

Modern science provides insight about the physical body that resonates with the Buddhist perspective. According to Dr. Jonas Frisén, a Swedish molecular biologist, the body's cells replace themselves every seven to ten years. During that span of time, our old cells die off and are replaced by new ones.[2] This clearly demonstrates that the body has no inherent existence and is always changing. When I heard about this research, I was reminded of a Tibetan story. An old man was on his deathbed. A friend came to visit and asked how he was doing. He replied, "I am doing fine, but there is an old man on my bed, and he is in a lot of pain." This dying man did not identify himself with his body!

Am I My Mind?

The third question is "Am I my mind?" To answer this question, we should first look at our feelings, the second of the five aggregates. Our feelings are generally categorized as either pleasant, unpleasant, or neutral. In other words, we may feel drawn to something, repelled by it, or indifferent to it. Our pleasant and unpleasant feelings provoke different emotions.

The word emotion derives from the Latin *emovere*, which means "to stir" or "to agitate." Emotions stir up something in us, motivating us to act in ways that are either constructive or destructive. Therefore, before investigating whether "I" is the mind, we should first check our behavior and see which emotions are there. Do you see one or more of the "five poisons" of anger, jealousy, pride, craving, or ignorance? Try to see this clearly. Then, when you investigate whichever negative emotion you find, do you see any judgment of yourself or others? If so, who is judging? Do you see where you have a blind spot? Can you see what is happening in your mind that you weren't previously aware of?

When afflictive emotions are transformed, we see our thoughts and perceptions more clearly. We recognize that our understanding of self is influenced by social relations and conventions. We also see how these social influences shape the ways we think, feel, and act. By transforming our negative emotions, we gain the insight necessary to transform how we live our everyday lives, and particularly how we relate to other people and to ourselves.

So which one is the real you? Are you your name, your title, your income, your social relations, your body, your thoughts, your feelings? Are you the labels associated with you? Does your height or weight, your wealth or rank, define who you are? You can take one step further to include all the adjectives you use to describe yourself. Are you tidy or messy, skinny or chubby, quiet or loud?

There is a misunderstanding that in Buddhism the self does not exist. This is not true. Saying that the self does not exist is the extreme position of nihilism. But we also want to avoid the opposite extreme that says the self does exist. That sounds tricky, right? How can we be beyond these two extremes? The key is that the self does not exist as an intrinsic, permanent, independent essence; if it did, it could never change and grow. But the self does exist in dependence upon an ever-changing body, mind, and environment. When we refer to "I," we refer to that collection of aggregates that we designate as our self, just as when we say "car" we refer to the collection of parts that we drive to the store. Neither exists independently, but both appear and both function. Therefore, what we take to be "I" is not a solid, independent entity but a flux of physical and mental events that permits us to function in society, in my case to be a brother and father, a teacher and abbot.

When we cling to the idea of self, we freeze it as if it were a solid entity, a static snapshot. But the idea of a solid self continually runs up against the reality that the self is really a process, a dynamic flow of phenomena. When we examine our mind through meditation, we start to recognize this reality; rather than grasping tightly to our idea of being a fixed "I," we relax into the spaciousness and openness of our actual nature.

Freedom from Ego-Clinging

A 2013 research study from the University of Texas at Austin suggests that people who say "I" more often than average correspondingly lack self-confidence.[3] The Buddhist perspective offers a simple explanation for this finding. When we have a strong ego— meaning we cling tightly to a sense of being an all-important, inherent self—we invite all kinds of mental afflictions such as jealousy, fear, greed, and anger. These mental afflictions perpetually destabilize our inner dignity. Having a strong ego makes it more likely that we hold on to habitual patterns, making it almost impossible to see our pure nature.

The assumption that a powerful ego is required to succeed in our highly competitive modern world is based on confusion over who we are. We see this in the two kinds of mirrors I mentioned before. Recall that the image the child first identifies with in the physical mirror becomes the seed for her self-image. That image relates to who we become as social beings. But the mirror of the heart, the one we contact through direct experience in meditation, reflects our genuine nature. This is the mirror that holds our deepest aspirations. To really know ourselves and connect with the openness, decisiveness, and freedom inherent in our inner dignity, we need to make a distinction between the relative me (the socially constructed self) and the real me (my genuine nature). The fact is that the less influenced we are by our socially constructed ego, the easier it is to live with true dignity and its abundant good qualities and strengths.

The fragility of ego destabilizes dignity. A friend who is a long-time Buddhist practitioner recently confided in me an incident in which she experienced the suffering caused by unwittingly clinging to ego. Linda, as I'll call her, was attending a Buddhist conference. At first, she felt calm and open-hearted. During a discussion session, the chairperson went clockwise around the circle of seated participants to make introductions. But after introducing the person to Linda's left, he then introduced the person to her right as though Linda wasn't there. She was stunned and became stressed. Many thoughts flooded her mind, each of which she found powerful, surprising, and embarrassing.

Feeling rejected, Linda became angry at the chairperson but soon turned the anger toward herself. She was disappointed in herself for having reacted that way. For years, Linda had practiced noticing her ego and letting go of clinging to the idea that she is a singular, independent, enduring self. And yet this incident provoked her ego into trying to defend itself. Fortunately, that defense played out only in her mind; she resisted the urge to say or do something in response.

It is of vital importance to know that learning about the self, as both a belief and an experience, takes time. And doing so is not a straight line. Our ego develops strong habits over time and repeatedly reinforces them. These habits have different layers that we can come to recognize through our practice. The outer layer of egoic habit is driven by a chattering, chaotic mind that is oblivious to our inherent awareness. Underneath this frenetic mental activity, moving to a subtler level of the mind, we can identify the grasping that propels our thoughts and actions. Beyond these two layers is our true nature. At this deepest, ultimate level, we no longer desire to protect and preserve the self. Working with these levels and learning to let go of ego is a dynamic process. Because our ego's habitual patterns are so deep and old, the residual ego-clinging resurfaces time and again when provoked. We should not feel discouraged by this.

Recognizing when and how our ego traps us is a positive sign. It is not a failure. It is transformation. It shows we are making progress on the journey of learning about ourselves. That is huge progress, really. If my friend Linda had not been a practitioner, she might have become depressed. Instead, she noticed her reaction and went on to practice recovering from it quickly. She was aware of exactly who, or what, was feeling hurt or offended. She also knew that when she investigated who or what the self is, she couldn't find it. Her negative experience was short-lived, as it should be, because she did not cling to the experience or beat herself up!

This incident, though difficult while it happened, became an opportunity for Linda to know herself more deeply. She had been so upset at being passed over in the introductions that she couldn't hear anything the other participants said during the panel discussion. This defeated her main purpose for being there. After a while, when her ego-clinging relaxed, she realized that her self-centeredness had been a magnet for her own suffering and a cause for furthering her alienation from others.

If we pay attention, we will see how our ego affects us in many situations in daily life. We don't have to be controlled by ego. We have a choice. We can relax our ego-clinging by investigating who this "I" is and where this "I" resides. When we don't find an answer, we slowly calm down. If we practice like this daily, we will gain understanding of emptiness, and certainty in it.

It is important to realize that emptiness is not a blank nothingness—it is open awareness. In this open awareness, nothing exists on its own or abides in a permanent way. This is true for all phenomena, whether our self-identity, a thought, an emotion, a car—anything. Phenomena arise due to interwoven causes and conditions, and therefore they are imbued with infinite possibilities. When we recognize the nature of mind, we see that everything arises from emptiness and dissolves back into emptiness. It is simple and beautiful.

Looking Deeply into the Self

The ego's habitual patterns reflect a kind of blindness. We fail to see how clinging to our self and giving it priority alienates us from others and generates suffering. The root of this condition is the duality that sees self and other as separate. Without an "other," there could be no "I." Self and other are wholly interdependent. Nothing exists by itself. We can learn to stop fixating on the dualistic thinking that separates "I" from "other" and to recognize that this "I" is merely a convenient label that we impute to the five aggregates so that we can function in relative reality. That is, we can come to realize that the self exists only in dependence upon the body, mind, and environment.

Our habit of seeing "I" as separate and apart from "other" is very deeply rooted. So are the habitual patterns that develop as a result over time. That's why we so easily are offended when someone says something insulting to us, or we feel small when a situation doesn't align with our sense of self-importance. When such feelings arise, we tend to react negatively, which only serves to reinforce the patterns that led to those feelings in the first place. We're caught in a cycle. We can break this cycle, but it takes time and practice to loosen our grip on the notion of being a solid self, and to develop insight into the interdependent nature of all phenomena.

A simple story of a conversation between the Buddha and his students may help us understand how this kind of insight develops progressively.

Three students went to the Buddha to ask about hell. The first student said, "I am really afraid of hell. What should I do?"

"Yes, hell is very scary," the Buddha replied.

The student then asked where hell is. The Buddha said, "It is many miles below the earth."

The second student came, asking the Buddha the same question. "Where is hell?" he asked.

"It is not up, and it is not down. Hell is a reflection of your anger," the Buddha answered.

The third student came, also expressing his fear of hell. The Buddha said, "Let me ask you a question. You said, 'I am afraid of hell.' Who is 'I'? Where is this 'I' that you are referring to?"

The third student pondered these questions for a while. He came back to see the Buddha and said, "I tried to find the 'I' and where the 'I' is located. But I cannot find it."

The Buddha laughed, "If you cannot find 'I,' why do you need to be afraid of going to hell?"

The Buddha gave three different answers to the same question because each student had a different level of clinging. The first student was strongly fixated on his belief in the self. Telling him that hell does not exist would not help him. For the second student, self-clinging was reflected in the emotion of anger. Therefore, the Buddha gave an answer to help him reflect on his own mind and free himself from the torment of afflictive emotions. The third student was ready to investigate where the self is. The Buddha gave the student what he needed to start analyzing who and where the "I" is. Pursuing this kind of analysis would eventually lead him to realize that all phenomena are impermanent, interdependent, and devoid of solid existence. After realizing this, he could then embark on experiencing it directly.

At one level, this story illustrates the Buddha's use of skillful means in responding to students' questions according to what they need to gain liberation. But it also illustrates the progressive levels of realization each of us needs to traverse for ourselves. First, we must loosen our grip on the strong belief in being a solid, singular self. Second, we must deal with our negative emotions. Finally, we can embark on the journey of exploring where and what "I" is.

The eventual result of this investigation will be discovering that who I am is my pure nature. Dignity is the quality that manifests when we identify with that pure nature rather than with our name, body, or mind. This nature is pure awareness. If we recognize it, we recognize ourselves, as if for the first time. But of course, we have never been separated from ourselves. We are simply getting to know ourselves for who we truly are. What we eventually find is the immeasurable richness of our genuine home and the basis for all positive qualities.

――――――――― DIGNITY TRAINING ―――――――――

Analytic Meditation

Begin by sitting in meditation posture. Spend a few minutes cultivating a calm and peaceful mind. When you experience inner calmness, start to explore who you are:

> Ask yourself: "Am I my name?" After reflecting on this for a while, go further to consider all the roles, titles, and attributes you associate with yourself. "Am I a student?" "Am I a sister?" Of course, at one level you are, but go deeper. Maybe you have a title or degree next to your name. Is that who you are? Maybe you think of yourself as tall, or short. Beautiful, or ugly. Is this really who you are? When you move past identification with these labels, then who are you? Do you feel freer when you don't affix labels to yourself?

> Then ask: "Am I my body?" Become aware of the feeling of being a self. You feel this, but where does it reside in the body? Can you locate it in the brain? In

the heart? Maybe the skin, hair, bones, or muscles? Is it in the molecules or atoms that make up the body? Is it the collection of all these smaller and larger parts? Can you ultimately find the location of the self?

> Then ask yourself: "Am I my mind?" In the same way that the body is constantly replacing its cells, the mind is a constant stream of fleeting thoughts, feelings, and sensations. Where is the self in all of that? For that matter, where is this mind? Does it have a color or shape? Is it inside or outside the body? Can you find the self anywhere in the mind?

> You may be surprised to be meditating in a way that involves thinking. The key to analytic meditation is that while we do think about the question at hand, we don't grasp at the thoughts that arise in response. If you can keep a sense of spaciousness, you will see that every thought that goes through your mind arises out of emptiness and naturally dissolves back into emptiness. The thoughts appear when the causes and conditions produce them and naturally disappear when the causes and conditions are no longer there.

> It is important to remember that this analysis does not require an answer. The point is to loosen our strong grasp on a solid idea of self. In fact, at some point during your analysis, when you are unable to locate the self, thoughts might naturally disappear. When that happens, let yourself rest in that state of empty awareness. Now you are experiencing the actual answer to the question. But it takes time to move from experience to actualization. Discursive thoughts will return; when they do, take up the analysis again.

> The purpose of this exercise is to first gain understanding of emptiness through analysis and then deepen that

understanding through experience. Emptiness means that phenomena are empty of independent existence. In other words, all phenomena are impermanent and interdependent—nothing has tangible, independent existence. Understanding emptiness will help you develop a more accurate understanding of yourself and of reality. When you let go of your erroneous perception of self and its byproduct of ego-clinging, you gain contact with your original, pure, self-awareness wisdom. You become less rigid about who and what you are, which brings more flexibility and happiness, and allows your inner dignity to manifest.

Inspirational Support

The question is not whether or not the person, personality or ego is a changing, composite train of events conditioned by many complex factors. Any rational analysis shows us that this is the case. The question is why then do we behave emotionally as if it were lasting, single and independent. Thus, when looking for the self it is very important to remember it is an emotional response that one is examining. When one responds to events as if one had a self, for example, when one feels very hurt or offended, one should ask oneself who or what exactly is feeling hurt or offended.

KHENPO TSULTRIM GYAMTSO RINPOCHE[4]

The Compassion to Act

Every man must decide whether he will
walk in the light of creative altruism or in
the darkness of destructive selfishness.

MARTIN LUTHER KING JR.[1]

In 2017, I was invited to coteach a Medicine and Compassion retreat for medical professionals in Jackson Hole, Wyoming. Dr. David Shlim, my co-teacher and the retreat organizer, is a long-time student of my grandfather Tulku Urgyen Rinpoche and my uncle Chökyi Nyima Rinpoche. Alongside his long and distinguished career as a travel medicine doctor and researcher, Dr. Shlim has passionately taught and written about the need to bring compassion into the field of medicine for many years. In 2000, Dr. Shlim initiated the world's first conference on medicine and compassion, and seventeen years later he organized this, the first in a series of annual Medicine and Compassion retreats.

Organizing any retreat is tremendous work, and an annual series is a particularly huge undertaking. Dr. Shlim could have continued comfortably writing and lecturing, but something happened to bring a new sense of urgency and purpose to his medicine and compassion project.

Two years prior to the first retreat, Dr. Shlim's son suffered a seizure. The seizure itself was not a big problem, but it caused him to fall onto a concrete floor, injuring his head. He was knocked unconscious; a scan revealed bleeding in his brain that required surgery. On a wintry day with heavy snow, he was evacuated from Wyoming to Idaho in a small airplane. It was five hours from the time of the seizure before Dr. Shlim's son finally made it to surgery, not an optimal situation for such a serious condition. Then, after so much frenetic effort and coordination, the waiting began. Following the surgery, standing by his son's bedside, not knowing whether he would live or die, Dr. Shlim felt tremendous suffering.

Two years before his son's accident, Dr. Shlim had experienced his own brush with mortality. He had suffered a heart attack while skiing on a mountain pass and had to be evacuated to this same hospital in Idaho. Although on that occasion his Buddhist training had helped to prepare him for the possibility of dying, in this instance he discovered that he was not at all prepared for the prospect of losing his son. In his great suffering, he suddenly thought of all who suffer in a similar way. Whether someone is in an earthquake or a car accident, or is a victim of violence or sudden illness, there is someone close to that person who suffers in the same way that Dr. Shlim experienced in that moment. And the sheer amount of suffering in the world is vast. For example, there are countless individuals and families in Syria, Iran, Afghanistan, India, and Africa dealing with famine, poverty, disease, and war. Truly, compassion must not be limited to the ones we love but directed to all beings.

Fortunately, Dr. Shlim's son survived and recovered. Even so, this incident made a big impact on his subsequent motivation. Despite having given many talks and written on the topic of medicine and compassion, Dr. Shlim felt called to make an even larger impact on the world. He started envisioning an annual retreat designed to actively enhance compassion in the medical community. Although compassion is widely recognized as important in health care, the medical field provides little professional training in its development. In fact, he found that there was no tradition for training in compassion at all. By contrast, Dr. Shlim had learned a great deal about compassion from his Tibetan Buddhist teachers, and he wanted to make such insights ever more available to the field of medicine. This retreat would contribute to this effort, with the intention of benefiting both medical professionals and their patients.

Turning aspiration into action, the 2017 Medicine and Compassion retreat became a reality. Dr. Shlim based the retreat on the 2004 book he cowrote with my uncle Chökyi Nyima Rinpoche entitled *Medicine and Compassion*.[2] My uncle was too busy to participate in the first retreat, so Dr. Shlim asked me. Given my interest in the topic and fortunate timing with my schedule, I accepted. Circumstances came together for me to coteach the retreat with Dr. Shlim two years in a row.

We rely so much on physicians and other health-care professionals to care for us when we go through the four rivers of suffering—birth, old age, sickness, and death. This is the reason why the Buddhist tradition holds the field of medicine and its doctors in such high esteem. These retreats were gratifying experiences for all involved. Even though we explored compassion in the specific context of providing medical care, the lessons learned apply more generally to all of life.

Compassion in Medicine and Buddhism

A group of medical professionals from all over North America arrived at the retreat location in the serene Teton Range, an isolated ranch nestled between Grand Teton National Park and Yellowstone National Park. It was fascinating for me to meet such a wide variety of medical professionals, including family medicine doctors, ICU doctors, psychiatrists, nurses, and pediatricians, among others. Each day I gave teachings on compassion from the Buddhist perspective before engaging in question-and-answer dialogue. These sessions provided a window into the North American medical profession, about which I previously knew little. The participants raised excellent questions while sharing their professional struggles. I was particularly interested to learn about the obstacles preventing health-care professionals from putting their compassion into action. It was quite evident to me that Buddhist practice holds great potential for guiding them in their professional as well as personal lives.

It is interesting how closely aligned Buddhism is with the practice of medicine. As I mentioned earlier, many Buddhist sutras compare the Buddha to a physician who diagnoses the problem (dukkha or suffering), provides the etiology or cause of the problem (ego-clinging), offers a prognosis (suffering can be overcome, you can recover), and points to the medicine for getting well (the Buddhist path). You may recognize these as the famous Four Noble Truths that most people have heard of. When you look at it in this light, it becomes obvious that Buddhism shares the same general goal as medicine—to identify and alleviate suffering.

The similarities between medicine and Buddhism extend to their ethical principles. Medicine states its commitment to alleviating suffering in one of its oldest texts, the *Hippocratic Oath* of ancient Greece. This document provides the code of conduct for the medical profession. In taking this oath, physicians pledge that, according to the best of their abilities and judgment, they will prescribe only beneficial treatments. They vow to refrain from doing harm and to lead exemplary personal and professional lives. Similarly, one of the guiding principles of the Buddha's teachings states, "Commit not a single misdeed; cultivate a wealth of virtue; completely tame your mind." Both traditions take a vow to benefit others while cultivating oneself.

Given these similarities and the nature of the work, I had expected the medical profession to emphasize training in compassion the way Buddhism does. I was surprised to learn that even though the *Hippocratic Oath* makes compassion a foundational principle, medical schools give this topic minimal attention. Consequently, medical professionals receive limited opportunity to increase compassion. Perhaps this accounts for why in a 2011 survey only slightly more than half (53%) of hospitalized patients reported having experienced compassionate care.[3] How much higher could this percentage be with proper training?

Compassion Fatigue: A Misconception

A hotly debated topic at both retreats I taught was a notion called "compassion fatigue." I was told journalists had initially coined this term in the early 1990s to describe nurses whose demanding work had left them drained of energy. This simple descriptor caught on and became widespread as a consensus portrait of the struggles of health-care professionals. Apparently, nowadays there is even mandatory training in compassion fatigue in US military mental health facilities.

It is true that much compassionate activity is hard work. Many physicians, nurses, social workers, and environmental and human rights activists can attest to this. Health-care professionals, for example, might become exhausted from working long hours and caring for more patients than their time and energy can handle. They may work in dysfunctional institutions, and their patients may be in tremendous pain. This can leave them physically and emotionally exhausted, a state commonly referred to as "burnout." As one retreat participant said, health-care workers can become so tired that they no longer take joy in seeing and helping their patients. But is this compassion fatigue? Or is it simply fatigue?

The term "compassion fatigue" conveys a misconception. Genuine compassion and fatigue do not go together. Compassion cannot become fatigued. It is our genuine nature to want to help others. Our genuine compassion can become blocked or covered up, but not fatigued. When we feel we don't care anymore—that we cannot care anymore—that doesn't mean our compassion is drained like a used-up battery. It simply means "I am tired" or "I don't have the energy to help others right now." This is not the same as saying, "I have lost all ability to care for others." This statement cannot be true. We cannot lose our nature. If we rely on a notion like "compassion fatigue," we might adopt or perpetuate a distorted understanding of ourselves, our nature, and our efforts.

Fatigue in health care is not always due to external circumstances alone. I have met many good-hearted, well-meaning health-care providers who are themselves emotionally vulnerable. Their good-heartedness lacks stability and strength. Many of us are easily affected by others' misery, and it is especially difficult in the medical industry. Sometimes the roles reverse so that it is the caregiver who needs care. I have pondered why this happens. Outwardly it seems as if they are being bullied by their circumstances, but really, they need to stand up to their own mental state—they must face their own mind.

I have heard that *empathy* is a popular term in medical schools. Empathy is the capacity to feel what another person is feeling, and it is a wonderful quality. But if we only feel what another person is feeling, we will suffer as much as they do, and this may leave us as incapacitated as they are. Then how can we help? Compassion is different from empathy. With compassion we understand and relate to the other person's suffering without withering in the face of it. Understanding another person's suffering motivates us to help them, and dignity and wisdom enable us to do that effectively. Therefore, we need to cultivate dignity and wisdom alongside compassion. Only then will compassion become steady, strong, and healthy.

What can we do when we are physically or mentally exhausted? We can acknowledge our experience, look directly at it, and learn from it. As we sit with it, we can see more and more deeply into the causes and conditions of our exhaustion. We might come to recognize that we are not suffering from "compassion fatigue," but rather we've been trying to practice compassion without dignity. We haven't been centered in our genuine nature. Compassion without dignity is not stable, nor is it genuine. Like dignity, compassion is an innate potential which can never be lost, even as we can lose contact with it. Like dignity, it is something we can cultivate.

Resilient Compassion: A Demonstrated Quality

Some people seem to demonstrate genuine compassion naturally, without effort. Their compassion is stable and resilient in the face of other people's suffering. One retreat participant shared an exchange he had with his surgeon mentor. He said this mentor is generally recognized as the most compassionate person in the hospital where he works. He asked him how he can always be compassionate.

His mentor answered, "I really want to help people. That's why I went into medicine."

"Well, why do you want to help people?"

His mentor answered, "How else would you be?"

This story of the irrepressibly compassionate surgeon generated engaging discussion among retreat participants as to why some people seem to be more compassionate than others. One person said, "It's the brain." Another jumped in, "It's genetic." These explanations suggest that our physical bodies establish limits on what is possible for our compassion. But it turns out that science has started to provide evidence that this is not the case. This conversation reminded me of the research conducted by neuroscientist Dr. Richard Davidson and his team at the University of Wisconsin in Madison starting in the 1990s and continuing today.

With the support of His Holiness the Dalai Lama, Dr. Davidson and his colleagues began using state-of-the-art scanning equipment to examine activity in the brains of advanced Buddhist meditators. The study participants were monks who over the course of their lives had meditated for tens of thousands of hours. Among them was one of my uncles, Yongey Mingyur Rinpoche. The scientists wondered whether the brains of these advanced meditators might look different from the brains of nonmeditators. That is, could meditation in any way affect the brain?

Dr. Davidson's team's findings were quite astonishing to the scientific community. While meditating on pure compassion—compassion without a specific object—the brains of participants showed extreme activation in those areas associated with happiness and well-being. Apparently, these areas were significantly more active than ever seen in nonmeditators, and they remained at least partially elevated when not meditating. This result affirms the Buddhist notion that our greatest happiness comes from love and compassion. For the scientists, it suggests that compassion is a "trait" rather than merely a "state."[4] In other words, compassion is a durable skill that can be cultivated rather than a passing experience that leaves no trace. Another way they state it is that our compassion baseline can be raised.[5]

Before these studies, scientists were convinced that for adults the brain determines experience. Now they are taking seriously a concept termed *neuroplasticity*—that experience can change the brain. In this case, the evidence suggests that meditation can rewire the brain, and compassion meditation can make us robustly happy.

But you may be wondering, what about those who don't have time to meditate for tens of thousands of lifetime hours? More recent studies have shown that even a little bit of compassion meditation goes a long way. For example, Dr. Helen Weng, a member of Dr. Davidson's team, found that study participants who practiced compassion meditation for only two weeks showed greater resilience in the face of suffering than those who did not. While looking at images of suffering, they were not compelled to glance away as people normally do, and the areas of the brain associated with negative emotions showed reduced activity. By taking study participants through a set of progressively extreme images of suffering, she demonstrated that compassion can be developed like strengthening a muscle or learning a new hobby.[6]

Additional research by Dr. Davidson's team has produced evidence that meditating on love and compassion produces neural patterns more resonant with the suffering of others, making us more likely to help. It also stabilizes our attention and reduces mind-wandering, particularly thoughts of self-obsession. As we continue meditating over the course of time, these and other qualities strengthen in us so that we transform in a robust way. This includes a reduction in the secretion of cortisol, a hormone that is activated by stress. These findings suggest that cultivating compassion is more than simply a useful skill for medical professionals— it is arguably essential. And not only for medical professionals but also for law enforcement officers, first responders, and anyone who helps others. And of course, we all want to help others, whether we recognize it or not. Everyone can learn to have compassion without fatigue.

Pride: Obstacle to Genuine Compassion

The topic of pride came up during both Medicine and Compassion retreats that I cotaught. I learned that pride is a common issue in the health-care community, especially among physicians. An ICU doctor confessed his challenges with feeling pride when he helps a patient. Everything in the ICU happens quickly and decisions must be made swiftly. He said that providing a correct diagnosis for a patient in such intense circumstances immediately brings up a feeling of great pride. But then, he continued, "Somehow this pride is always followed by a nagging feeling of anger, and then fear." He called his feelings "medicine pride."

When we do a good deed, we know it deep in our heart. This is how it should be—there is nothing wrong about feeling good when saving lives. But we should ask ourselves: What is the driving force of our action? Do we help others because they need help? Or do we help others so that we can feel good about ourselves? In other words, is our compassionate act about us, or is it about others? Do we put ourselves first, or do we put others first?

I've heard a saying that "helping is its own reward." I agree with this. When we help someone, we should simply be happy that the person has been helped. But pride gives us a sense of ownership. It is as if pride and ownership were two sides of one coin. When we help someone and pride arises, we believe that we "own" compassion. Compassion becomes about me, not so much about the other person. I am happy because "I" helped you. Compassion without ownership is genuine compassion because it reflects our genuine nature. This makes it unconditional. When we say "I" saved someone, our identification with "I" is strong, which makes our compassion automatically weak. Doing that is a problem.

The stronger our ego, the weaker our compassion. When we humbly and sincerely desire to benefit others, our compassion strengthens. When thinking we are superior to the people we help and taking pride in our actions, we are unable to give in a sincere way. Our goodness is good only until we attach to it. When we attach to our good actions, pride surges and compassion declines. As we discussed in the previous chapter, we cannot avoid using the word "I" altogether. We must communicate. But it is important to think of the "I" not as the ego but the bearer of our compassionate aspiration and responsibility. It comes from a deeper place.

The self-centered superiority of pride is based on comparison. Comparison robs us of a full understanding of others and reality. It makes our compassion segmented or compartmentalized. Due to pride, our giving discriminates between "good" beneficiaries and "bad" beneficiaries, between rich and poor, friends and enemies, Americans and non-Americans. For example, it is very common to have compassion for people living in poverty without recognizing that rich people deserve compassion too. While people with low incomes suffer a lack of material comfort, rich people have other kinds of suffering. With pride we segment our compassion based on our own projections and expectations rather than the actual needs of others. In this way, our compassion is limited, conditional, diluted, and incomplete. It does not have the strength and beauty of the genuine compassion taught by the Buddha.

We sometimes see this distortion of compassion among political activists. Many activists regard anger as a necessary and unavoidable driving force for their activism. They don't see that their anger is pride in disguise. The Zen master Thich Nhat Hanh has observed that the peace movement in America during the 1960s had no peace itself because people quickly became angry.[7] Beneath their anger was the pride of thinking that others were wrong while they were right, and that those others must be destroyed accordingly. We often forget the compassion that drove us to action in the first place. We fixate on self-centeredness and divide friends from enemies. Unfortunately, this ego-based attitude alienates us from our dignity, enforces our distorted projections, and separates us from others. We forget that we are interconnected with all beings. Then we become part of the problem that we wish to correct.

Pride arises when we identify with our illusory ego; dignity arises when we identify with our innate nature, our inherent goodness. Compassion can be genuine only when it is based on dignity. This is what makes compassionate action strong and steady. Compassion grounded in dignity has no agenda. We don't act in expectation of receiving anything in exchange. We are focused wholly on the benefit of the other person. But to the extent we identify with ego, and pride is involved, our compassion has strings attached. We want something for ourselves.

Of course, there usually is a trace of pride in our compassion. Realize that pride is only a habit; we are habituated to thinking that we are more than others, which ironically deprives us of our full power. By strengthening our dignity, our original nature, we work toward reducing and eventually eliminating all traces of pride. This means we work toward increasing our positive qualities and reducing our negative ones. Dignity is always humble, but pride never is. Dignity adapts to any situation, but pride cannot. Dignity notices, but pride judges. Dignity is not affected by mistakes, but pride is. With dignity, we steadfastly seek to improve ourselves. This makes it possible to notice our blind spots and address them. Rather than hiding from our faults, we face them head on and correct them.

When we base compassion on dignity rather than pride, our fears and insecurities are reduced. We recognize our interconnectedness with all beings, and equality becomes a guiding principle. Rather than protecting ourselves, we seek to protect others. Compassion grounded in dignity guides us like a moral compass, whereas pride makes us moral police. Until we are enlightened, we cannot completely rid ourselves of pride, and we will know its presence when we become emotional, dissatisfied, afraid, and easily fatigued. Confronting the challenges posed by negative emotions such as pride is a long process. But it is a rewarding step that we must take if we aspire to live a more compassionate life.

Putting Compassion into Action

Mahayana Buddhism considers compassion to be the essence of bodhicitta. Earlier, I described bodhicitta as the sincere wish to help other beings overcome suffering and attain enlightenment. This is also known as "relative bodhicitta," because it maintains a sense of relationality between a helper and the person being helped. Inseparable from relative bodhicitta is "absolute bodhicitta," which is the realization of emptiness. This realization transcends the notion of a helper and someone being helped. I will have more to say about that soon, but for now, let's concentrate on relative bodhicitta.

Recall that relative bodhicitta has two divisions: aspiration bodhicitta and application bodhicitta. When we practice the four immeasurables—love, compassion, joy, and equanimity—we are practicing aspiration bodhicitta. We make aspirations that turn our focus away from self-centeredness and open our hearts. We can also practice the "six paramitas" as a way of putting these aspirations into action. This is how we practice application bodhicitta.

The Sanskrit word *paramita* translates as "perfection." By practicing the six paramitas and applying them in our daily lives, we transcend our usual habitual patterns and perfect our compassion, wisdom, and dignity. The first five paramitas—generosity, discipline, patience, diligence, and concentration—relate to relative bodhicitta, while the sixth one, wisdom, is the wisdom that knows emptiness. The six paramitas are a huge topic, but I would like to briefly mention them in the context of our discussion on compassion.

When we practice generosity, the first paramita, we actively give to others. We're all familiar with giving material things such as food or gifts to friends, family, or those in need. Other important forms of generosity include preserving life and giving nonmaterial things such as our presence or our loving and compassionate advice.

Discipline, the second paramita, does not mean being rigid or inflexible, which we tend to associate with this word. In this context, discipline is simply being responsible for our actions. To do that we must be mindful to do no harm and to benefit others. Making this commitment serves to align our actions with our fundamental dignity so that they arise from a genuinely compassionate motivation.

Patience, the third paramita, has several levels. When confronted with challenging situations, we first need the patience of not reacting. Then we need the patience of understanding those who make us suffer. The next level is the patience of taking difficulties as the path. Without patience, we react, or overreact, and then we surrender to doubt instead of cultivating compassionate understanding. For any compassionate action, patience is indispensable.

The fourth paramita, diligence, is an action performed with joy and good motivation; it is sometimes called "joyful effort."

Perfecting the fifth paramita, meditative concentration, means that our mind does not waver from awareness. We remain mindful of what we are doing and aware of ourselves and what is going on around us.

The sixth paramita, wisdom, is the absolute bodhicitta I mentioned earlier. This is the realization of emptiness that makes the other paramitas "transcendent." In fact, sometimes the six paramitas are called the "transcendent perfections." When we combine generosity, discipline, patience, diligence, and concentration with the wisdom that knows emptiness, then transcendent or absolute compassion becomes possible. For example, when we give money to a beggar (the first paramita), ego remains involved until we can perform it without a sense of there being someone giving, someone receiving, something being given, and an act of giving. When we can give without being constrained by any of these concepts, then our generosity is transcendent. It becomes a pure expression of our inherently generous nature. The same principle applies to the other paramitas. In this way, the six paramitas cultivate our innate compassion, wisdom, and dignity.

The six paramitas are well known in Buddhism. Less well known are the "ten paramitas." These consist of the six paramitas plus four additional ones representing further aspects of the wisdom paramita: skillful means, strength, aspiration, and primordial wisdom. They provide further support in making the other paramitas transcendent.

For example, if you throw money at a beggar, are you giving with generosity? I think not. This is the reason why generosity needs skillful means, the seventh paramita. The Tibetan word that translates as "skillful means" is *top*, meaning "very good at." We need to be good at giving. Generosity also needs strength, the eighth paramita. Without strength, we may be worn out by our actions. Aspiration (*monlam* in Tibetan), the ninth paramita, keeps our intention alive, while the tenth, primordial wisdom (*yeshe* in Tibetan), permits us to act with ultimate wisdom. *Ye* means "primordial," and *she* means "always present." This wisdom has always been present with us and is always available.

These additional paramitas remind us to not cling to the act of giving or to having any expectation in return. Otherwise, our generosity becomes diluted or impure, and we may find ourselves with regret later. For example, if you offer $200 to a charity but then later regret the donation, thinking you should have given only $100, your initial generous intention is polluted. Giving with calculation is not generosity; it reflects your stinginess, which is the opposite of generosity. The same principle applies to the other paramitas.

Have you noticed that practicing compassion is relatively easy when everything in your life is going well? In contrast, how is your compassion practice when you are experiencing physical, emotional, or financial difficulties or when your self-image is being challenged? Compassion is not true compassion if it does not transcend our habitual tendencies or emotions. In other words, compassion must be based on an understanding of emptiness or egolessness. Without this understanding, our practice of compassion is not a paramita (perfection). Of course, until we are enlightened, our compassion is partial and not perfect. But practicing these paramitas will lead us in the right direction as we cultivate and strengthen our inherent qualities of compassion, wisdom, and dignity.

Stability and Inclusiveness

In his last teaching, Jigme Phuntsok Rinpoche famously said, "Do not lose your ground. Do not disturb other people's minds." I find these parting words very powerful. Although some choose to translate the first sentence as "Do not lose your path," my preferred translation—"Do not lose your ground"—makes evident that Phuntsok Rinpoche is reminding us never to lose contact with our buddha-nature, the ground of our compassion. This ground is the same for all of us, no matter who we are. When we lose our ground, we abandon our aspiration to benefit others. We must not run away from difficulties when they arise—we must be brave and decisive and maintain our ground. Then we ensure that our compassion is stable.

Phuntsok Rinpoche's next words of advice, "Do not disturb other people's minds," is the core of compassion. We disturb others' minds whenever we make them angry or upset or when we use divisive speech. Being determined never to disturb anyone's mind, no matter who they are, makes our compassion inclusive, without discriminating between rich or poor, young or old, people of one nation or people of another. When we maintain our ground, and the aspiration to never disturb anyone's mind, our engaged compassion becomes effortless, and we make progress in actually alleviating suffering. It is a habit to wander off from our ground, our buddha-nature, but if we always remember to return, this habit will weaken. We will never feel lost, and our compassion will expand and grow.

We can find many contemporary examples showing the benefit of not losing one's ground and not disturbing the minds of others. The lived experience of Garchen Rinpoche is one such example.

Garchen Rinpoche is a highly revered lama in the Drikung Kagyu lineage of Tibetan Buddhism. During the Chinese Cultural Revolution, he was captured, imprisoned, and confined to labor camps. During his twenty years' imprisonment, he met Khenpo Munsel, a fellow prisoner who became his root guru. Khenpo Munsel's teachings helped Garchen Rinpoche endure unfathomable hardships. In Garchen Rinpoche's own words:

In the beginning, prison to me was the world of hell. In the middle, after I met Khenpo Munsel Rinpoche, the hard labor which I had thought as painful and fruitless ever so slowly became my daily Dharma practice. At the end . . . prison became like a land of jewels, and the hatred and anger toward my enemies ended up being completely transformed.[8]

Garchen Rinpoche never lost his ground and never disturbed the minds of others, including the minds of the prison guards who tortured him. Since his release from prison in 1979, he has worked tirelessly to teach compassion.

Garchen Rinpoche exemplifies the two mental qualities of true compassion: stability and inclusiveness. He said, "I didn't return from the prison empty-handed. Suffering, the source of pain, became the catalyst. I was able to develop genuine altruistic aspiration . . . and through that, to fulfill the purpose of my human birth in this lifetime."[9]

The mere fact that Garchen Rinpoche survived so many years of imprisonment and torture is incredible enough. That he used this experience as opportunity to dramatically increase his compassion is awe-inspiring. His compassion encompasses the entire world, including himself and the prison guards, and no one can take it away from him. Through the quality of his great compassion, he has gained liberation from positioning himself against others, and he works tirelessly to protect everyone.

DIGNITY TRAINING

Tonglen: The Art of Giving and Taking

The Tibetan word *tonglen* translates as "giving and taking," or "sending and receiving." It is sometimes also known as "exchanging self with others." Tonglen is a compassion meditation in which we mentally take on or receive the suffering of others while giving or sending them our peace and happiness. This sounds counter-intuitive, and from the perspective of ego, it is. But deliberately exchanging our favorable circumstances for the suffering of others transforms our limited compassion into great compassion. Our heart becomes pure, simple, gentle, humble, open, and vast. It returns to its original beauty and purity. In the process, we not only help to heal others, but we also heal ourselves.

You might feel hesitant to do this practice, but don't worry. Breathing in others' suffering will not harm you. It is only from ego's perspective that you will seem to be sacrificing your own well-being. On the contrary, you are the primary beneficiary of this practice. As you shift focus from yourself to others, your innate qualities of love and compassion will be awakened and strengthened. Your negative habits will be reduced. Your sense of ownership ("my compassion," "my success," "my practice") will lessen. You will develop the qualities of stability and inclusiveness, eventually being ready to help the world as a real bodhisattva.

The following preparatory practice reduces attachment to yourself. You will feel lighter and readier to do the practice of giving and taking.

> Calm your mind using one of the earlier breathing techniques. A calm and clear mind is essential before you can exchange yourself with others.
> Next, contemplate the equality of all beings. If you are struggling with fear, worry, or sickness, think of the countless others enduring similar suffering at this very moment—just as you wish to be free from suffering, so do they. On the other hand, if you are feeling joyful

and happy, think of how all beings would like to feel this same happiness—just as you wish to be happy, so do they. We all share the same attitude toward suffering and happiness. Why should one individual's happiness be more important than that of others?

> Imagine your ego as a black ball in the center of your heart. Visualize that it is sucking in and absorbing all your negative thoughts such as grasping, anger, jealousy, fear, and attachment.

> Then visualize that this black ball explodes and dissolves into thin air without leaving a trace. Notice any difference you may feel.

> Now we come to the tonglen practice itself, which is very simple. Basically, you mentally give away your happiness and take in others' suffering. Coordinate this process of giving and taking with your breath. You can do this practice with a particular individual, with a group of individuals, or with all beings.

> As you exhale, visualize all your positive qualities and good fortune as cool light spreading out to all suffering beings. In this way, offer them your happiness, good health, joy, loving-kindness, wisdom, and realization.

> As you inhale, breathe in all their pain, discomfort, fear, illness, depression, and fatigue while wishing them freedom from all suffering.

> After repeating this process for as long as you choose, conclude your practice in silent meditation. Allow the distinction between self and other, between giver and receiver, to naturally dissolve. Rest in the spaciousness of emptiness. Now you have moved from the relative compassion practice of tonglen to the absolute compassion practice of resting in the natural state.

Take your time with this practice. Don't rush. At first, it will require deliberate effort and may feel artificial. It might not feel genuine to send others your happiness and good fortune while receiving their pain and suffering. It is all right to feel that way at the beginning. This practice will enable you to slowly recover your long-lost deep connection with all beings, animal and human alike. This is part of recovering the innate purity of your compassionate nature.

Inspirational Support

> All the joy the world contains
> Has come through wishing happiness for others.
> All the misery the world contains
> Has come through wanting pleasure for oneself.
>
> SHANTIDEVA[10]

Part
Three

Gaining Certainty
and Trust

Know by yourself your own
supreme self-awareness.

TILOPA[1]

Authentic Power

If you are free, you need to free somebody
else. If you have some power, then your
job is to empower somebody else.

TONI MORRISON[1]

Before he became the Buddha, Siddhartha Gautama grew up as
a prince—a son of the ruler of the Sakya clan. Before Siddhartha's birth, a holy man prophesied that the young prince would
become either a great king or a great spiritual leader. Siddhartha's
father wanted his son to inherit his worldly power and become
a king. But Siddhartha disobeyed his father and gave up worldly
power in pursuit of the spiritual path.

Which of these options would you choose? Would you pursue
being a world leader or a spiritual leader? To have worldly power
or spiritual power? Why? Take a moment to consider this.

A professor friend usually begins her introductory lecture on
Buddhism with this story before asking her students the very
question I just asked you. Most of her students say they would
choose worldly power, arguing that possessing financial, military,
or political power is the best way to solve the world's problems.

"You must have money and power to be able to help others," they assert. These eager young people want to do something good for the world. The question is how many of them would be able to convert that initial intention into concrete action that is truly beneficial.

These students see power in the same way most of society does—as a form of control that extends beyond oneself. This includes control over other individuals, the state, or society. Such control is usually accompanied by personal success such as wealth, social status, fame, and physical strength. We become very busy climbing material, social, and political ladders, but does this kind of success and power bring us happiness? Is there a risk that we may become so consumed by external goals that we don't pay enough attention to what is going on inside us?

I have met wealthy and famous people whose inner lives are filled with struggle and suffering. For many, the desire for worldly power or fame easily overrides altruistic motivation, leaving them impoverished inside. But there is another kind of power than the kind that controls what is happening outside oneself. This is the power that controls what is happening inside oneself—the power of one's inner life. From a Buddhist perspective, inner power is much greater than external power. Why? Our perception of the outer world depends on the quality of our mind. It is only through the exercise of inner power that we can bring outer power to bear in positive and beneficial ways.

What is the basis of inner power? Dignity. Inner power naturally manifests when we recognize and fully dwell in our originally pure nature, our inherent goodness. With dignity, we can exercise outer power in wise and beneficial ways; without dignity, outer power becomes tremendously seductive to the ego, threatening to exercise control over us. When we fully dwell in ego, we perceive outer power as its own reward, divorced from inner values. We become preoccupied with what "I" like, what

"I" think, what "I" want. We may begin with good intentions, but such intentions are easily corrupted by external pursuits.

At best, external power is unstable. At worst, it may incite trouble and disharmony. The spiritual power of dignity is rooted in awareness and decisiveness. When we have worldly power, our compassion and wisdom may or may not always manifest. When our mind is not calm and peaceful, we may fail to use power with compassion and wisdom. But when we have dignity, our compassion and wisdom radiate naturally; we become naturally powerful. True power is inherent in us; we need only learn how to access it.

Imagine a society full of compassionate, healthy, and insightful individuals. Wouldn't it bring powerful, revolutionary change in the world, organically?

Compassion, Wisdom, Dignity

The Tibetan Buddhist tradition often compares compassion and wisdom to the two wings of a bird. Just as a bird needs two wings to fly, we need both compassion and wisdom to transform the mind. Having compassion without wisdom, we will nosedive. Likewise, having wisdom without compassion, we will nosedive. We cannot have one without the other. It's a nice analogy, right?

But there is a third element considered essential in the Tibetan Buddhist tradition. That third element is dignity. If we were to play with the traditional analogy, we could say that two wings alone are not sufficient to prevent us from nosediving—we also need the power to flap our wings. This is how we move forward.

Therefore, to fly properly—meaning to fully transform ourselves and help others—we need compassion, wisdom, and dignity. All three are essential. If we lack one, our efforts will not be effective. We must cultivate all three of these qualities alongside one another.

At the same time, each of these qualities is complete by itself. When compassion is genuine, it is naturally imbued with both wisdom and dignity. Similarly, wisdom is imbued with compassion and dignity, and dignity with compassion and wisdom. When we encounter someone who naturally radiates wisdom and compassion, we notice that they also exude stability and strength, the qualities of dignity. It could not be any other way. Such a person has become stable in the recognition of their intrinsic nature. Arriving at that point requires that we work on compassion, wisdom, and dignity alongside one another.

It is very instructive to see how Buddha Shakyamuni taught these qualities. He taught compassion first. To love is so natural. It is easier for us to experience deep connection with other sentient beings and feel their suffering than it is to immediately examine ourselves. In teaching compassion, the Buddha taught awareness of our interconnectedness with all beings, including humans, animals, plants, and minerals.

Next, the Buddha taught the nature of suffering and the nature of self. We develop wisdom through insight that the self is not permanent and is composed of parts.

After that, the Buddha taught dignity, or vajra pride. The ultimate understanding of compassion and wisdom is that they are our innate nature, which is never separated from us. What can we learn from the way the Buddha taught these three essential and interrelated qualities? Let me put it this way:

Compassion is how to begin.
Wisdom is how to develop.
Dignity is how to be.

We begin by working with our own emotions and having some caring for others. We develop further by understanding the self and its illusory nature, which allows us to clearly see both our faults and our inner qualities. This clear seeing is the wisdom that enables us to distinguish between what to do and what not to do. We know how to be to the extent that we have confidence in our innate qualities, our primordial wisdom. We have the dignity to be ourselves and to remain true to who we are.

Three Protectors

Please do not think that we do compassion meditation to develop compassion, wisdom meditation to develop wisdom, and dignity meditation to develop dignity, as if these are separate trainings for separate qualities. It does not work like that. No matter what kind of meditation you do or how long you do it, every instruction in the Buddhist teachings generates all three qualities. The three qualities of compassion, wisdom, and dignity are so intimately interconnected that they often are grouped together to represent our most precious qualities. This collection of three qualities is sometimes known as the "three protectors." They protect us from the harm of mental and emotional confusion. So long as we have all three, we are protected, no matter the circumstance.

Perhaps you have seen images of Tibetan Buddhist art, such as those displayed at the Rubin Museum of Art in New York City, or in magazines or books. Tibetan art frequently depicts different buddhas with a wide variety of appearances. Some look rather "normal" with peaceful expressions, while others look fierce or angry, with many arms and legs. Although these images may look alien to us, they represent our own intrinsic qualities. How can you depict compassion? It is not exactly something you can see. What about wisdom? Again, you can't see it. Or dignity? You can know it, but not see it. Tibetan Buddhist art symbolically depicts these and other "invisible" qualities using iconic images.

Compassion, wisdom, and dignity are represented by the buddhas named Avalokiteshvara, Manjushri, and Vajrapani.

Although buddhas, they are often also referred to as bodhisattvas to highlight their extraordinary bodhicitta. Each symbolizes one of the buddhas' qualities: Avalokiteshvara is the embodiment of the compassion of all buddhas; Manjushri is the embodiment of the wisdom of all buddhas; and Vajrapani is the embodiment of the dignity of all buddhas. These three beings are sometimes said to have surrounded Buddha Shakyamuni as protectors of the inner treasure of awakened nature. But we can understand them as the qualities we need to protect ourselves from confusion. What does it mean to call these protectors "buddhas"?

As you may recall, the term *buddha* means "awakened one." What kinds of beings are awakened? Being awakened means having complete compassion, complete wisdom, and complete dignity. You may ask what it means to call these qualities "complete." It means that they are not partial or based on opinion. And they are not something we own. Compassion is not "my" compassion or "your" compassion. Wisdom is not "my" wisdom or "your" wisdom. Dignity is not "my" dignity or "your" dignity.

Genuine compassion, wisdom, and dignity are like the sun that shines everywhere equally, without discrimination. We must go beyond our tendency to put ourselves first or to see things from "our" point of view—to think that our compassion is the correct compassion. Compassion is simply compassion. Wisdom is simply wisdom. Dignity is simply dignity.

The buddha that represents compassion, Avalokiteshvara, is one of the most popular and beloved figures in the Buddhist world. Although usually depicted as male, Avalokiteshvara takes the female form of Guanyin in the Chinese Buddhist tradition. In Tibetan iconography, Avalokiteshvara has many symbolic representations. The two most typical are one with four arms and another with one thousand arms. Both are white in color, symbolizing the pure compassion of the heart. The four arms represent the four immeasurable qualities of compassion, loving-kindness, joy, and equanimity.

The one thousand arms represent the tireless activities of bodhisattvas reaching out to help everyone in the universe. Each hand has an eye in its palm, which symbolizes how compassion (the extended arm) is always guided by wisdom (the eye).

Manjushri is considered the bodhisattva of wisdom—another popular figure in Buddhism. He is depicted as yellow or gold in color, representing the sun shining on everyone equally. His right hand holds a sword—the sword of insight that cuts through doubt and ego. His left hand holds a lotus flower with a Tibetan-style book (*pecha*) on top. The book symbolizes blazing knowledge. From this representation, we know that wisdom is needed to cut through negative emotions as well as gain knowledge of egolessness. Real wisdom is letting go of fixation on ourselves, what we regard as ours, and what we think is right. Through the openness of wisdom, we access the essence of our nature. Cultivating wisdom requires that we work with our inner self, recognizing and developing our inner qualities. When we are confronted with obstacles, for example, we can use them as catalysts to overcome difficulties and develop wisdom. Once wisdom is developed, it cuts through ignorance.

The representative of dignity, Vajrapani, is well known in Tibetan Buddhism but less popular in other Buddhist traditions. Many times, Vajrapani appears as one of the fierce or "wrathful" deities with the quality of subduing negative emotions. He is blue like the sky, representing space. No matter how many clouds cover the sky, the sky is always there, pervasive and unchanging. In his right hand, Vajrapani holds a ritual implement called a *vajra*, signifying power and strength. The vajra is indestructible and unbreakable. It is the hardest material on earth; when the vajra is thrown, other things break but the vajra does not. Vajrapani's left hand holds a mirror at his heart. A flame arises from his left index finger, signifying that dignity blazes at the heart center. In Japan, Vajrapani is the inspiration for popular guardians called Niō (Benevolent Kings) standing majestically at the entrance of many Buddhist temples. Like Vajrapani, these guardians have a wrathful and frightening appearance, signifying their fierce power to subdue bad influences, remove obstacles, and protect good qualities.

Although each of these buddhas represents—or highlights— one of the three protector qualities, all three qualities are fully developed in each buddha. For example, although he might appear otherwise, Vajrapani is filled with love and compassion. His fierce and wrathful appearance represents the power of dignity to subdue the ignorance of ego-clinging and the negative emotions it generates. This is a wise and compassionate thing to do. Similarly, compassion and wisdom also subdue—compassion subdues anger, and wisdom subdues ignorance. Compassion, wisdom, and dignity are the three protectors shielding us against our habitual tendencies and confusion, using both peaceful and wrathful means.

The three protectors manifest in people's warmth of presence (compassion), sharp insight (wisdom), and inner power (dignity). As we have seen, these qualities are inseparable, and as such, dignity is essential. Anyone with stable compassion and wisdom is inherently powerful, and the power and stability of dignity make it possible to fully cultivate our compassion and wisdom. No matter how compassionate and wise we may be, without dignity it is difficult to transform ourselves in a genuine way. Human beings are not only compassion beings and wisdom beings but also dignity beings. We just need to recognize it. That is the most crucial way to maintain our inner treasures.

Is Dignity Ever Truly Lost?

Of course, developing genuine compassion, wisdom, and dignity is a process. We make plenty of mistakes along the way. This is understandable and natural. Our habits are longstanding and stubborn, and it takes time to reduce and eventually eliminate them. When we make an especially terrible mistake, something that we fear has caused harm to another person, our self-recrimination can be huge. It can prevent us from feeling inner freedom and living with a sense of dignity. This is a wretched feeling that traps us in a nightmare that won't go away.

A few years ago, a student told me about a regrettable mistake he had made years earlier. Unable to forgive himself, he had felt tormented ever since. He told me the following story:

A good friend of mine in high school couldn't admit to himself that he was gay. The world was quite conservative at that time, and many people believed that being gay was a disease. We remained in touch after graduation, though sparingly. One day, someone told me that my friend had recently gone through shock therapy. Soon after that, I received a letter from him telling me he had married. I wrote back to congratulate him and wish him happiness. A few months passed without hearing from him, so I wrote again. In this letter, I told him about my blissful experience of listening to Verdi's opera *La Traviata* on my two-hour drive home after a day of long meetings with my devious, power-seeking colleagues. I later realized that everything I had written was about myself—my happiness, my bitterness, my judgments. I was so full of myself. I didn't ask about my friend or his marriage at all.

It is commendable that this student recognized and admitted to his self-centeredness on that occasion. But then he confessed to his big mistake:

This time I received a letter in reply. It was from his wife. She informed me that my friend had killed himself. Even though I hadn't met his wife, I could tell from her letter that she was warm and kind. I don't know what came over me. My next move was unforgivable. I wrote her back, saying that I had been very surprised he'd married a woman.

Continuing, the student said, with tears in his eyes, that later he thought to himself: "What have I done! Why did I act so unkindly?" He then told me, "After realizing what I had done, I found myself despicable. I had lost all respect for myself. I had lost my dignity."

For many years, the student identified with his faults and could not forgive himself. In this sense, he lost his dignity because he lost contact with his buddha-nature. If he had recognized that his mistake was a mistake of the ego, which is not who he really is, then he could have made amends in time. Instead, his deep regret left him living in confusion and pain, preventing him from moving forward.

Our capacity to change comes from recognizing the fundamental purity of our nature. When we lose contact with that nature, it can feel as though the gravity of our actions is irreversible, rendering no possibility for change. In this student's mind, he was stuck in his past mistakes and could not live with dignity.

We must remember that when we feel that we "lose our dignity," our dignity is never actually lost. Dignity, or vajra pride, is an inherent quality of our fundamental nature. It is always present. What we have lost is contact with our dignity. The regret, shame, and sadness that lurk at the edges of our lives may cloud over our dignity, temporarily. But only temporarily. The Tibetan Buddhist tradition identifies a set of techniques to purify our past mistakes.

Because these techniques are so powerful, they are often referred to as the "four powers." These four powers enable us to amend our mistakes and restore our relationship to ourselves. We break identification with our mistakes while resolving never to commit them again.

Four Healing Powers

The four powers for purifying our mistakes are the powers of (1) remorse, (2) support, (3) commitment, and (4) antidote. Each of these powers is essential in the process of reclaiming contact with our dignity.

The Power of Remorse

First and foremost is the power of remorse, as illustrated in the Buddhist tradition by the story of Angulimala. As a young man, Angulimala was tricked by his jealous classmates, and as a result he set out on a mission to kill 1,000 people. After killing 999, he started to have doubts. Then he encountered the Buddha, who guided him to use his heartfelt remorse as the basis for purification and transformation.

The story of Angulimala became an example of how anyone, even in the most extreme circumstances, can find redemption by giving up what is unwholesome and transforming regret into compassion and wisdom. Interestingly, the Buddhist prison chaplaincy in the United Kingdom is named Angulimala, the Buddhist Prison Chaplaincy. This organization uses the story of Angulimala to inspire inmates by showing that change, and enlightenment, is always possible, no matter the severity of one's past negative actions.

Without genuine remorse, we cannot transform our negative actions into positive ones. We must first acknowledge our actions, recognize the harm they have caused, and really feel that. We generally commit negative actions without thinking about their consequences, and then our ego does everything it can to keep us from really looking at that. When we feel genuine remorse, however, we have overcome our ignorance and fully accepted responsibility for our error. It might hurt at first, but this is the only way change is truly possible.

In writing the letter to his friend's widow, the student didn't initially recognize the harm he was creating. But being a person of good heart, later he did. When he realized what he had done, he felt tremendous remorse. Unlike Angulimala, the Buddha wasn't there to guide him through the process of working with his remorse. He didn't know that he could use his remorse to make amends for his negative action, forgive himself, and transform his mind. And he didn't know that the problem was that his remorse was mixed with feelings of guilt and shame.

You might be surprised that the first time I heard the word *guilt*, I did not understand it. There is no such word or concept in the Tibetan language. Intrigued, I asked my American students to explain it to me. They told me that guilt is a feeling that there is something fundamentally wrong with you. I was shocked. Because of guilt, people feel ashamed not only for their mistakes but even more for their own existence. They think, "I am such a terrible person. I am unworthy." In such a moment, they have lost all contact with dignity. They see no possibility to change their future actions because they believe they are intrinsically bad. There is no hope. This way of thinking can easily lead to self-hatred or depression.

From the Buddhist perspective, beating ourselves up with guilt only serves to reify the ego. In this way, guilt is its own form of self-centeredness. To believe that we are fundamentally guilty and flawed ignores the fact that our nature is pure. A good heart can make mistakes, and with the right understanding, a good heart can purify them. Far from uplifting us, guilt paralyzes us and prevents us from accepting ourselves as we really are. With guilt, we are unable to make a realistic appraisal of our situation, and we may find ourselves frozen with self-loathing.

In contrast, genuine remorse, not entangled with guilt and shame, has the quality of purifying. Remorse means that you recognize that something you have done is a mistake, you see the suffering that has arisen because of your mistake, and you vow never to repeat that mistake.

Sometimes the terms "remorse" and "regret" are used interchangeably, but they have slightly different meanings. We tend to regret an action that limits our personal potential, such as dropping out of school. But we typically wouldn't feel remorse for dropping out of school. And while we might also regret causing harm to another person, remorse is different. Having remorse comes out of a sense of personal accountability and taking stock of oneself. If we only "regret" saying a bad thing to someone, then we may not yet feel remorse. If we feel remorse, we are genuinely concerned about the negative impact our words and actions have had on others. We feel bad and want to rectify the situation. Remorse, when it is genuine, inspires the determination to correct our mistakes and never repeat them in the future. This is how we reconnect with our fundamental dignity.

The Power of Support

The second power is the power of support. There is a well-known practice in Tibetan Buddhism by which we confess our mistakes and purify them. It is called Vajrasattva practice. Vajrasattva is a loving, caring, and trustworthy buddha to whom we direct our confession. His love, compassion, and nonjudgment support us in our efforts to purify our mistakes, whether intentional or unintentional. This practice requires guidance from an authentic teacher, but the idea behind it is universal. Therefore, please don't think you need to be a Buddhist or religious person to apply the power of support.

The power of support has inner and outer aspects, and we need both when facing the challenge of confronting our own mistakes. The outer power of support is someone who bears witness to what we have done, someone with an objective view of the situation. This should be someone we trust to see, hear, and understand us. Although Buddhists might rely on the felt presence of Vajrasattva, we can find support in a noble friend with the compassion and wisdom to help us reconnect with our intrinsic dignity. The inner power of support is to connect with our bodhicitta, our awakened heart. Working with our mind to develop immeasurable compassion weakens and dispels the suffering of loneliness and gives us tremendous perspective. We come to recognize that we are not defined by our mistakes, and we see clearly how to address them.

The student felt remorse after realizing what he'd done. He didn't tell anyone about it for a long time and was unable to find a way to alleviate his suffering. The outer and inner powers of support, when combined, provide us the clarity to see and address our life situations. This is very physically, psychologically, and emotionally healing.

The Power of Antidote

The third power is the power of antidote, meaning employing skillful methods to counteract the consequences of our mistakes and to make amends. This includes asking for forgiveness. In general, the antidote to nonvirtuous action is virtuous action. For example, those who have hurt loved ones by lying to them could deliberately speak about their deceit in an open and honest way. Someone who has caused harm by driving under the influence of alcohol could involve themselves in educational work that helps prevent others from making the same mistake. When we recognize that our lack of compassion has caused suffering in others, we commit to do the opposite—to cultivate love and compassion for their benefit. We do this in a form that has the effect of counteracting our negative actions. This is the power of antidote.

The Power of Commitment

The fourth power is the power of commitment. At this point we have felt remorse for our unskillful action, and we have sought support to gain clarity and reconnect with our fundamental dignity. We also have applied the power of antidote to counteract our negative action. The next step is vowing never to perform this harmful action again.

Of course, our mistakes usually come out of deeply entrenched habits, and at some level we realize this. So we might think, "But what if I can't uphold this vow? I'm afraid that I might fail. I don't think I can promise that." This is a common way of thinking, but this kind of hesitation guarantees that we stay stuck in our negative pattern. Vowing to not perform a harmful action in the future sets a positive and healthy intention, which itself is healing. If the negative pattern is deep, we may indeed fail in the future, but we also will be quicker to recognize, accept, and purify our mistake. As we repeat this process, the pattern will grow weaker and weaker until it no longer has any power over us. Such is the power of the four powers.

Although I've described the four powers sequentially, they all support one another. Still, healing can begin only when we feel remorse. In fact, when remorse is genuine and deep, it engenders the other three powers. For example, in remorse we bear witness to what we've done and the goodness of a heart that feels the way ours does. In this way, remorse provides its own power of support. Remorse is in part its own antidote insofar as the strong feelings we have serve to counteract what we've done. And genuine remorse always motivates us to refrain from performing the negative action again, which effectively enacts the power of commitment. Still, at a practical level, we need all four powers to play their mutually supportive roles in our healing and transformation.

Whichever way we work with these powers, the ingredient that makes them possible is our inner dignity. We may lose contact with our dignity, but it is always there. Our mind is fundamentally pure, healthy, and positive. Mistakes and negative actions are impermanent; we are only ever temporarily lost. By applying the four powers, we heal our sorrows, reduce our negative patterns, and realign with our dignity. I encourage you to apply these powers to any of your own past mistakes that might haunt you. We all make mistakes, and we can always transform them.

Decisiveness

Only when we come to know dignity as our basic nature can we let go of our doubt, uncertainty, and insecurity. Only then can we develop the decisiveness required to transform ourselves and change the world. We usually are submerged in the mistakes we've made and distracted by strong and negative thoughts. It is important to learn to bring our doubts and negative emotions to cessation. Without such cessation, we continue cycling through the habit of condemning ourselves and feeling there is something wrong with us.

Decisiveness means having no doubts or regrets and being willing to change. We often don't trust ourselves, and so we do things with one foot in and one foot out—in a halfhearted way. Why are we not fully committed? Usually, we are terrified of criticism. Even if we can see our own flaws, when someone else criticizes us, we become weak and unsteady. We lose contact with our dignity. Is it possible to hear criticism without attaching to it? Maybe there is something in what our critic is saying that we need to change, or maybe we are not being perceived correctly—either way, there is no problem, only an opportunity to know ourselves better. Adopting such an attitude requires a basic willingness and commitment to improve and change. Then we can accept and take responsibility for our flaws or mistakes without taking others' criticisms too personally. In this sense, decisiveness means acceptance—accepting who we are, who others are, and how the world is. And we accept that we will make mistakes and do our best to correct them.

"Accepting who we are" sounds cliché, and maybe on the surface it is. But the deeper meaning is not. It is a common misunderstanding that accepting who we are is the equivalent of accepting our habits. This is not what I mean. Our habits are both good and bad, and they are constantly shifting and changing. If we think we are our habits, the ground is always shifting beneath us.

Having a good heart and an understanding of emptiness will not in themselves solve our problems—we must have confidence in our nature. Confidence in our nature is true confidence in who we are. When we know our nature, mistakes don't bother us in the same way. We make mistakes, confess those mistakes, and we change. It becomes very simple and sane. There is no guilt or self-recrimination. When we reach this point, everything is decisive. There is a common belief that people become wiser as they age. But that is not guaranteed. Without making the effort to change, to be decisive, I don't think we can be wise, no matter our age.

To be decisive, we must encourage ourselves and know what needs to be improved. Know your vulnerabilities. Notice, without judging. Focus on nature, not habits. Pursue compassionate happiness, not selfish happiness. Most importantly, the mind must be stable and undistracted. When undistracted, the mind is clear and calm. With decisiveness as our basis, we naturally develop stable and inspiring presence.

Being decisive is not a religious idea; it relates to our human condition. It is an important quality for functioning in life. People who make clear decisions with the goal of benefiting and not harming others have an elegant, steady presence. Such presence is a sign of good leadership. It is known as *ziji* in Tibetan. *Zi* means "shine." *Ji* indicates "magnificence." The magnificent shine of ziji is the expression of gentle richness that arises when we have confidence without aggression. It is a result of being decisive, of trusting in ourselves and the world.

When we gain trust and certainty in ourselves, we cannot help but want to do something beneficial for the world. The world does not orbit around the ego anymore. Ego is an actor, always in the theater. When we discover our innate dignity, we no longer need to act. We only need to be who we really are—compassionate, kind, and dignified.

———————— DIGNITY TRAINING ————————

Open Awareness

Begin by sitting in a comfortable position, keeping your posture straight and eyes gently open.

Make your mind as vast as the sky. When a thought or feeling arises, such as worry, anger, or judgment, notice it as though it is a tiny bird in the vast sky. Do not follow it. Do not attend to it. Simply know that the tiny bird has flown into the space of the mind, and it will fly out of the space of the mind.

Without focusing on anything, rest in the vast spaciousness of the mind with full awareness. You are inseparable from the clarity and spaciousness of mind. Thoughts and feelings, those tiny birds, come and go, but they cannot affect you. They come, they go, and the mind remains in a state of openness—calm, relaxed, undistracted, and aware.

Rest and let yourself be in that state.

Inspirational Support

Simply observe your awareness in this very present moment, just as it is. It cannot be spoiled by the comings and goings of thoughts and memories, nor corrupted by ordinary thoughts of good and bad. There is something here that is at once both vivid, yet devoid of thoughts; devoid of thoughts, yet vivid.

THE THIRD DZOGCHEN RINPOCHE[2]

Dignified Living and Dying

We die, and we do not die.

SHUNRYU SUZUKI[1]

Over the years, I have frequently been asked, "Rinpoche, how can I die with dignity?" I usually give a simple answer: "To die with dignity, we must live with dignity." How we die has everything to do with how we live. Therefore, in teaching us how to live with dignity, this book has also been teaching us how to die with dignity. But now we must consider the topic of death from the other side. Thinking about death has a powerful effect on how we live. In other words, contemplating death helps us to cultivate dignity.

I understand these words may be unsettling. The topic of death is taboo in many cultures, particularly in the west. Even though death is a natural part of life, many of us resist thinking about it. Of course, intellectually we know that once born, we will certainly die, but it is difficult to let this reality sink into our hearts. The uncertainty about when and how we will die frightens us. Even worse, having no clue as to what happens after we die presents a terrifying unknown. Some people are so haunted by the thought of death that they forget to live, and others so preoccupied with living that they forget that they will die. Either way, without a healthy and balanced regard for death, it is difficult to live a meaningful life.

What Is Death?

We ordinarily associate death with the moment our physical body stops functioning. But death is much more pervasive than that. From a Buddhist perspective, death occurs in every moment—and so does birth. For example, the cells in our body are constantly dying as new cells are constantly born. Each breath that we take must end so that a new breath can begin. Thoughts and emotions constantly arise and constantly cease. Yesterday dies, and today is born. In every moment of every day, we experience death, continuously and constantly—but rarely are we aware of this. Therefore, it is helpful from time to time to reflect on the pervasive presence and necessary role of death in our lives.

The event we conventionally designate as death, when our heart stops beating and our lungs stop breathing, is as inevitable as it is unpredictable. If our body does not expire prematurely, it eventually grows old, succumbs to illness, and stops working. In the Buddhist view, when the physical body eventually does expire, the mind does not. The mind continues. In this context, the word *life* means that both our body and our mind are alive, whereas "death" means the physical body has ceased to function while the mind continues.

When our physical body expires, we find ourselves separated from all we have held dear in our lives, including family, friends, wealth, and possessions. Therefore, all that we value and treasure in life, including all that we have acquired, is for us as imperma-nent as our body. We arrive in the world empty-handed, and we exit the world empty-handed. But, again, the mind or conscious-ness does not die—it continues. This larger perspective gives us a different way of thinking about death. It casts death as simply the transition of consciousness. And it turns out that this transition is a precious opportunity for transformation.

For those who believe that death ends in oblivion, the pros-pect of dying is horrifying and must be avoided at all costs. The Buddha taught that our basic nature continues after death, along with the habitual patterns of our consciousness. Therefore, after our current life ends, we will continue to experience countless states of existence, one after another. In this sense, it is an illusion that death is the end of life. This is the reason why Buddhism emphasizes the importance of training the mind. All the good qualities we cultivate in this life—calmness, freedom from grasp-ing, loving-kindness, compassion, and wisdom—will continue in our mindstream long after our present physical body is gone. We have the opportunity and means to develop these qualities in this lifetime—we must value this life and not waste it!

The True Meaning of Dying with Dignity in Buddhism

When we are dying, our physical body grows weak, and our senses start failing. Eventually, our eyes cannot see, and our ears cannot hear. What will help us when this moment comes? This is important for us to consider now, while we can. At the time of dying, the knowledge we have acquired in life will not help us. The books we have read will not come to our assistance. The possessions and wealth we've acquired will be of no value what-soever. There is little our friends and family will be able to do for us. All we can rely on is our own mind.

It is therefore very important to gain familiarity with our mind and its innate nature, deepening our connection with who we really are. This is the essence of living with dignity. We train to live with dignity by cultivating the qualities of decisiveness, confidence, and nonattachment. During the dying process, we carry these qualities with us. This is the true meaning of dying with dignity.

I must distinguish between what the Buddha taught about dying with dignity and the premise behind the Death with Dignity Act, a bill passed in Oregon in 1997 to legalize physician-assisted suicide. In the context of the Death with Dignity Act, the dying process itself is seen as an indignity from which we may choose to free ourselves through suicide. The Buddhist perspective is that the dying process—even though it can be very difficult—is an opportunity to strengthen our dignity. Life is precious, and the human body is precious; therefore, we should make every effort to not die. If only heroic and impractical medical measures are keeping us alive with no hope of recovery or a meaningful life, then we can consider discontinuing treatment and dying a natural death. But we are advised to never actively take our own life. When we have exhausted all practical remedies to continue living, we prepare to die without regret or fear, and possibly to die even with joy. This is dying with dignity.

Those who believe that death is merely a transition of consciousness tend to be less attached to their bodies, families, and possessions. They regard dying as part of life—whatever arises will eventually pass. They recognize how crucial the moment of death is. In the moment of dying, we have a final opportunity to shift our identity from ego-self to buddha-nature. If successful, there is a real possibility of reaching enlightenment. With this as our aspiration, our eventual death becomes a precious opportunity rather than something to fear and avoid. The prospect of actualizing enlightenment at the time of dying has everything to do with having cultivated dignity at the time of living.

What does enlightenment mean? Enlightenment means we have actualized our buddha-nature, which also means we have actualized our dignity. Enlightenment means we have overcome our basic sense of alienation to simply be who we have always been. Enlightenment means being 100 percent kind and pure, with no agenda born of projection. Enlightenment means having complete certainty and trust without so much as the possibility of wavering, doubt, or hesitation. Because our dying moments hold great potential for enlightenment, from the Buddhist perspective, preparing for the end of life is not, strictly speaking, preparing for death—it is preparing for enlightenment.

Inspiring Examples

There are many instances of individuals who have died with dignity and without fear. I have directly witnessed some of these and heard numerous stories of others. My grandmother is one such example. She died from pancreatic cancer, which I was told is very painful. But my grandmother always exuded positive emotions and never exhibited signs of pain or suffering.

Another good example is Khandro Lhamo, the wife of Dilgo Khyentse Rinpoche, one of the preeminent Tibetan Buddhist masters of the twentieth century. Khandro Lhamo was an accomplished doctor of Tibetan medicine and an extraordinary practitioner. Even so, she was very humble. During her last few years before passing away, she gave most of her few personal belongings to lamas with whom she was close. These possessions included small diamond earrings, rings, and other items. She also donated all the money she had collected during her lifetime to the rebuilding of Shechen Monastery in Tibet. These actions were part of her preparation for death.

Right before Khandro Lhamo passed away, the doctors were panicked. But Khandro Lhamo was anything but panicked. She was accompanied by Rabjam Rinpoche, her grandson. Rabjam Rinpoche recalled how Khandro Lhamo looked at him and said with great joy, "Now I am dying, isn't that it?" She thought this was the funniest thing. "Ha ha ha," she laughed. "I am dying, aren't I?" She was perfectly happy and joyful.

Rabjam Rinpoche explained that in the Dzogchen tradition of Tibetan Buddhism, the death of a practitioner is like a daughter returning to her mother's house. In Tibet, when a daughter marries, she moves from her mother's house to that of her husband. There is so much joy when the daughter can finally return to her mother's home. This seemed to be what happened with Khandro Lhamo—the joy she expressed while passing was like that of returning to her mother's home.

After she passed, Khandro Lhamo's body remained warm for three days. In the Tibetan Buddhist tradition, this means that although her body had stopped functioning, her mind stayed in a meditative state called *tukdam*. Remaining in meditation like this after the body is clinically dead is a sign of a highly realized practitioner.

Khandro Lhamo indicated her wishes clearly and prepared for her death fully. The way she died demonstrated how she had lived, approaching death with humor and joy rather than regret and fear. The quality of her mind made it possible for her to die with dignity—and with laughter!

The Story of Martin

While it is not unusual for advanced Buddhist practitioners to die with dignity, it is also possible for anyone to die a dignified death. Martin was a student who was diagnosed with amyotrophic lateral sclerosis (ALS)—a notoriously debilitating and rapidly degenerative disease. The first symptom appeared when his tongue felt unusual. Then his speaking, eating, and drinking grew steadily more laborious. Three months after his diagnosis, he lost the ability to speak. Six months after that, he was on a feeding tube. ALS is a fatal disease; there is no cure. Death seemed to approach quickly. After the diagnosis, Martin started writing a blog called "My ALS Adventure," documenting the progression of his neurodegenerative condition. "I always liked adventures," he said.

Martin and I first met in Kathmandu where he had come to trek in the Himalayas. Then he became a regular attendee at the annual summer retreat I teach in upstate New York. After he became ill, he continued to come on retreat, even when he could no longer speak or eat normally.

On an unusually hot day, the retreat participants gathered for ice cream. One of them saw Martin walking by and shouted out to him, "Martin, come join us. We're having ice cream." She had forgotten that Martin's condition had progressed to the point that he couldn't take anything by mouth. Martin came over to join the group anyway. Despite his condition, he was at ease, always graceful, and never displayed any sign of dreariness or despair. He savored every remaining moment of his life.

Because he couldn't speak, Martin had to ask questions in writing, which encouraged him to ask fewer questions. But in his silence, Martin came to realize that most of the endless questions we distract ourselves with are irrelevant to what really matters. We forget that we must answer our own questions through our experience in meditation.

When friends asked him how his illness had affected his meditation practice, Martin answered with this:

> I feel even more blessed to be alive. Without my human body, I couldn't practice at all. And my mind can no longer pretend that my body will never die. Ordinarily, we rarely feel that every moment is precious because we only know intellectually that we will die.

When Martin knew he was actively dying, he said goodbye to a group of close friends via email. He also connected them with his loving wife, and he informed them about burial and funeral plans. In his final blog, he wrote:

I've done everything I can think of that I can still do. There's little I can learn by continuing to live like this, and I will become an ever-increasing physical burden to my beloved partner. So, I will eat and drink no more. I have been blessed in so many ways. Now I am excited to see what comes next.

During the dying process, Martin continued to practice with diligence until his physical body reached the end. Using his quickly advancing illness as the path, Martin prepared for death with dignity. He faced his illness and the process of dying with total acceptance and bravery. He died with no fear. Prior to death, he took care of his worldly responsibilities as best he could, and even while physically incapacitated he managed to touch many lives through his blog. As his parting gift to the world, Martin advised his son to keep his blog going so that it can continue to be helpful to others.[2]

At the end, nothing was left undone. Martin's physical body had run its course. With calmness and without regret, he exited this life. The way Martin prepared for death offered those who witnessed it a vivid demonstration of dying with dignity. Dying with dignity is possible for all of us.

Wisdom at the Time of Death

One of the most famous teachings in Mahayana Buddhism is called the *Heart Sutra*. This sutra offers the Buddha's profound view of the emptiness of all phenomena. Virtually everyone in Asia, whether

Buddhist or not, has heard of the *Heart Sutra*. But when I asked my students in Asia how to practice the *Heart Sutra*, they couldn't give me answer. This made me think of another Mahayana teaching called *The Noble Wisdom of the Time of Death Sutra*. This simple and beautiful teaching is a favorite of mine. It provides clear, pithy instructions on how to train the mind and prepare for death. Because it is extremely condensed, the language can be challenging; however, you have already encountered most of this content in our previous chapters. Still, if you find what follows difficult, you may want to take your time with it, or perhaps skip to the next section of the book and return later. The choice is yours.

The Noble Wisdom of the Time of Death Sutra consists of a very brief exchange between a bodhisattva named Akashagarbha and the Buddha.[3] In addressing the Buddha (whom he called Bhagavan), Akashagarbha asks: "Bhagavan, how should a bodhisattva regard the mind at the time of death?" The Buddha's reply comprises five brief verses that remind us of what we must remember at the time of death. These essential points are: (1) the view of emptiness, (2) the motivation of bodhicitta, (3) the meditation on profound emptiness, (4) the understanding of impermanence, and (5) the result or fruition that comes from that understanding. Remarkably, these brief verses cover the entire path for training the mind. Because these five points are so important and easy to apply, yet dense in their presentation, I briefly discuss them here.

Since phenomena are by nature pure,
Cultivate the notion of lack of existence.[4]

The first verse refers to the view of emptiness. "View" means a way of seeing or understanding. In the view of emptiness, all phenomena are naturally pure yet lack inherent existence. What does this mean? "Phenomena" refers to everything that can be named. All phenomena—whether mountains or musings, cars or emotions, images on a screen or in our heads—are not created by anyone but the mind that perceives them. Although we might confidently assert that our pen was created by the pen factory, looking more deeply, we must admit that the pen only appears to us because we have a mind to perceive it. Because all phenomena are inseparable from the mind, they are considered natural.

Phenomena are considered "pure" because the mind from which they arise is itself pure, as we have already discussed. The nature of mind is buddha-nature, meaning it is originally awake. Although we are temporarily obscured and confused, our nature is nevertheless pure. Similarly, even though we go around labeling whatever is arising in our field of experience—thereby creating a duality between this and that, subject and object, inner and outer—that doesn't mean the fundamental nature of whatever we experience is any less pure.

Next, this verse tells us that because phenomena are by nature pure, we should cultivate the notion of lack of existence. "Lack of existence" means that when we search for the mind, we cannot find it. Even though we experience having a mind, it doesn't exist. This may initially be a little difficult to understand. We can only truly understand the emptiness of mind through our own direct experience of it. Reading books or talking about our feelings won't be of much help. We must go inward and look directly at our own mind. Ask yourself, "Who is thinking? Where does this thinking come from? Where does it go?" Simply look at the mind. The moment you look, you won't find anything. That is the meaning of "lack of existence."

Since they are infused with bodhicitta,
Cultivate a mind of great compassion.[5]

The second verse refers to the vast motivation of bodhicitta. Recall that this motivation inspires us to benefit all beings without exception. In a way, all 84,000 of the Buddha's teachings are contained within bodhicitta, which is the combination of compassion and wisdom. Compassion relates to relative bodhicitta—such as the four immeasurables discussed earlier—while wisdom relates to absolute bodhicitta, the realization of emptiness. Because bodhicitta combines compassion and wisdom, the "great compassion" that we must cultivate is based on wisdom rather than ego; as such, it is the wish to awaken all beings to wisdom. If we take time from our busy lives to cultivate bodhicitta, our other meditation practices will progress quickly, including our practice on the nature of mind. Therefore, it is especially important to think of bodhicitta at the final moments of life, and to cultivate it well before then.

> *Since everything is naturally luminous,*
> *Cultivate a mind free of reference point.*[6]

The third verse refers to the meditation on profound emptiness. What is meant by everything being "naturally luminous"? As discussed earlier, when we look at our mind, we can't find anything. There is no place that the mind comes from, there is no place where it abides, and there is no place to which it goes. But that doesn't mean our mind is in a blank state. What we find instead is clear presence. This clear presence is often called "luminosity."

When we see beyond our ordinary state of mind, beyond all thoughts and emotions, we find that the mind is empty yet luminous. Upon recognizing the nature of mind, we have transcended the duality of subject and object. There is no concept of being a self that sees nor of an object being seen. The nature of mind is beyond any reference point, beyond any grasping, clinging, or elaboration. It is simply empty, clear, luminous awareness. We have returned home to our genuine nature. Therefore, true meditation is simply being without any doing.

Since all entities are impermanent,
Cultivate a state of mind that is free of attachment.[7]

The fourth verse implores us to understand that everything is impermanent so that we free our mind from attachment. Impermanence is not a theory or hypothesis; it is an inherent characteristic of all phenomena. Everything changes. Nothing remains unchanged from one moment to the next. This is what is meant by saying that everything is impermanent.

As we discussed earlier, we easily recognize the fact of impermanence intellectually, but we just as easily forget it in our day-to-day lives. When we forget impermanence, we become fixated on things, other people, situations, and our bodies as though they will last forever. Because we are living out of sync with the reality of the situation, our heart becomes anxious and hard. One of the many benefits of learning to constantly remember impermanence is that our heart softens. We relax our mistaken grip on things as fixed and permanent. We come to accept things as they are with more ease. We recognize that rather than being an enemy, impermanence is what makes transformation possible. It is impermanence that makes liberation possible. Once we understand impermanence, our mind will not be attached to any individual, object, or idea. Then we are truly free from attachments.

Mind is the cause for the arising of wisdom;
Don't search for buddha elsewhere![8]

The fifth and final verse is about the result or fruition that comes from realizing the first four points. This fruition is dignity. When the mind truly recognizes that everything is impermanent and that nothing lasts, then the mind is realized. Likewise, when the mind genuinely sees its nature, without a reference point, then the mind is realized. In other words, true wisdom is the mind seeing itself as wisdom. This true wisdom is the ultimate dignity.

The Noble Wisdom of the Time of Death Sutra provides the proper preparation for death in five steps: First, we establish the view, which serves like a lighthouse to guide us in the right direction. Then we cultivate the motivation, which makes us aware of why we act. Based on our view and motivation, we learn how to meditate. Next, developing understanding of impermanence loosens our attachments. Finally, going through the process of training like this yields the desired result.

One time, after I gave a teaching on this sutra, a student in the audience said, "The sutra is titled *Wisdom of the Time of Death*. Shouldn't we cultivate this wisdom during our entire life and not just do it at the time of death? When we are dying, we may be in too much pain and suffering to be able to contemplate these verses." This is so true. According to the commentaries on the sutra, we can apply this teaching both during the dying process and throughout our whole life. As soon as we are born, we are moving closer to death. Every moment is a chance to practice and prepare for death.

Contemplating these verses gives us a chance to acknowledge our innate capacity for transformation. It may be too late to learn this wisdom if we wait until our final stage of life. The only things that will help us at the time of death are the positive qualities we have cultivated over the course of our life. If we have cultivated a peaceful mind, we will die with a peaceful mind. If we have cultivated dignity, we will die with dignity.

I want to remind you again that this sutra will help us only if we study it, contemplate it, and, most important, put it into practice. Only then will we gain experience and benefit from this teaching. Merely understanding these verses as ideas will not help much. But if we maintain these points in our practice every day, a little bit at a time, it will really increase our dignity. And this will help us live and die with dignity.

The Value of Contemplating Death

Some people mistakenly think of meditation as a method that brings only joy and peace or makes us feel good about ourselves. But meditation should open us to all of life, including those aspects that aren't always pleasant. We cannot deny that old age, sickness, and death are natural processes. Death is an important and essential part of life, and we must give it our full attention. Avoiding the unavoidable only results in more terror and misery.

Although examining death may initially feel uncomfortable, if we stick with it, we will quickly start to realize major benefits. As we come to accept the reality and inevitability of death, we stop taking life for granted, which makes us feel more awake and alive. Recognizing that our time is limited and precious, we make wiser decisions about how we want to spend that time. We live life with a greater sense of purpose and meaning, adopting a conscious set of priorities. We recognize the importance of cultivating love, compassion, wisdom, and dignity. We gain the determination to live a dignified life for our own benefit and for the benefit of others. In short, as we lose our fear of death, we gain a deep appreciation for life.

──────────── DIGNITY TRAINING ────────────

Contemplating Death

> Assume a comfortable seated posture.
> Take a few calming breaths and let your mind settle.
> When you are calm and alert, loose and relaxed, proceed with the following three related contemplations.

During this process, hold your thoughts lightly. If they become too heavy—if you become overly anxious or otherwise worked up—bring your mind back to a state of calmness and begin again when you are ready.

1. *Death is certain.*

First, contemplate the certainty of death. Everything born will eventually die. This is true of inanimate objects as well as animate beings. For example, even mountains erode over time, eventually ceasing to be. Contemplating in this manner gives us a broad view of impermanence. Then consider all the people and animals that have ever lived. What a vast number that is. How many of them are still alive? Only a small percentage, and those people will all be dead in a few generations. Think of famous, larger-than-life people, such as your favorite writers, artists, philosophers, kings and queens, and so forth. They all die. Even great religious leaders die. All the people we know today will one day die. And, finally, you too will die. Contemplate this as a way of generating a living experience and conviction that death is real.

2. *The timing of death is uncertain.*

Having become somewhat convinced of the inevitability of death, contemplate the uncertainty of the timing of death. We often assume that death is in some remote future, especially if we are young. But how far off is that future, really? Of course, death may indeed be decades from now, but it could just as well be tomorrow. There is no way of knowing when and how you will die. Think of all the different possible causes of death and contemplate their unpredictability. Notice what arises in your experience as you contemplate this.

3. *What will help me at the time of death?*
   Knowing that you will die, and that the timing of your death is uncertain, now ask yourself, "What will help me at the time of death?" Will anything you have acquired or attached to in life help? For example, consider how you ordinarily spend your days and whether those activities will matter at all when you are dying. Will your hobbies benefit you? Will the possessions and wealth you have acquired benefit you? In short, what will help you at the time of death? This question assumes greater urgency to the extent your first contemplations have had an effect (which may take several sessions). We could also phrase this question as "What will help me to have a dignified death?"

> To conclude the practice, let all thinking go, and rest naturally.

If you have not had the opportunity to confront the reality of death, you may feel anxious about doing this exercise. A little anxiety is expected, but if your anxiety feels overwhelming, you may want to wait and return to this exercise in the future. If you want to continue, gently remind yourself that becoming more aware of death is a healing process. We can only overcome fear and anxiety around death by getting to know it, never by avoiding it. When the time arrives, death is a threshold we must cross alone. No one else can die for us. And only our mind accompanies us when we die. With this thought, reflect on the benefit of working with your mind and coming to recognize your own pure awareness.

Nothing ever stands still; from moment to moment everything is changing. In spring, seeds send out shoots; in summer, the shoots grow into leaves, stems, and flowers; in autumn, the grain ripens and is harvested; and in winter, the earth is again prepared to receive next year's crop. As the moon waxes and wanes over the course of a day, everything undergoes incessant change. Noon might see a thousand people singing and dancing in a fairground, yet dusk finds the whole place silent and empty. In the meantime, each one of those revelers will have slipped a few hours closer to death.

DILGO KHYENTSE RINPOCHE[9]

Carefree Ease

With great ease comes great meditation.
With middling ease comes middling meditation.
With lesser ease comes lesser meditation.

THE SECOND KARMAPA[1]

The whole purpose of meditation is to realize and stabilize our dignity, the essential quality of our pure nature. This dignity, or vajra pride, is like a diamond buried deep within the earth, and meditation is our means of revealing it. This takes effort. Whether studying and contemplating, focusing on the breath, cultivating love and compassion, or looking directly at thought, we are removing the obstacles that prevent our dignity from fully manifesting and unfolding. When this beautiful diamond finally appears from underneath the layers of dirt, we realize that it has never truly been sullied by whatever has obscured it.

Once we have mastered our mind, we can directly and effortlessly recognize our dignity. We don't need to flip a switch to turn it on. But in the meantime, our dignity must be cultivated. This cultivation can be approached in two ways: (1) based on mind and (2) based on wisdom. When we cultivate dignity based on mind, we try to understand how our mind works; when we cultivate dignity based on wisdom, dignity naturally unfolds by itself, free of effort. This effortless unfolding requires our mind to be already calm, stable, and open. When we maintain this state, awareness of buddha-nature spontaneously arises. At this stage, meditation and conduct are in perfect harmony. Our day-to-day interactions with others continually improve. We face challenging situations in calmer and more relaxed ways. We are free from self-centeredness and grasping. My teacher Soktse Rinpoche described this effortless state as "carefree ease" (*guyang lodey* in Tibetan).

"Rinpoche, carefree ease . . . carefree ease." Soktse Rinpoche often reminded me of this phrase. Here "carefree" means a heart that is wide open and not constricted; it does not mean being careless or irresponsible. A mind of "carefree ease" is vast, spacious as the sky, free of confusion and complexity, and utterly at ease—no matter what is happening in our lives. This concept is quite simple, simply because it describes our natural state. This reminder about carefree ease is one of the greatest pillars of my dignity practice. It is the principle that guides both my meditation and my conduct.

Without carefree ease, our dignity is like a rope tied in knots; with carefree ease, our dignity is like a snake that naturally uncoils itself. This reflects what happens when we live in accordance with our true nature. With carefree ease, our wisdom and compassion are stable, grounded in the decisive certainty that our nature is pure. This certainty makes it easy for us to acknowledge our mistakes and learn from them. Then we can quickly improve ourselves.

Right now, we don't recognize our dignity most of the time, but that is okay. Our dignity does not depend on whether we recognize it or not, and it doesn't change depending on whether we accept it or reject it. It is always present and always the same. Real dignity is completely natural, free of all concepts and completely fresh as it is. When we cultivate carefree ease, we can access our dignity twenty-four hours a day. Remaining in this state, we are free of all the weight we carry, all the suffering, pain, projects, responsibilities, and plans. The moment we dwell in our nature, everything is liberated. This is our genuine home, the genuine source of dignity.

Three Ways of Cultivating Carefree Ease

How do we cultivate carefree ease and find our way home? Remember that the Tibetan word for meditation, *gom*, means "to become familiar with." It doesn't mean to sit idly by doing nothing. Through meditation, we become familiar with who we really are and the nature of reality as it really is. We gain new ways of knowing and seeing that challenge our usual modes of understanding and perceiving. As we become familiar with our mind and our mind's nature, we naturally align with and come to know our inherent dignity. There are three principal ways of gaining this familiarity: (1) applying antidotes, (2) cutting through, and (3) self-liberating.

We previously discussed the first method, applying antidotes, in chapter 5. After we can recognize our emotions and start gaining familiarity with them, we apply the specific antidotes designed to transform specific emotions. For example, when anger arises, we apply the antidote of loving-kindness. When jealousy is present, we practice rejoicing. This method quickly transforms our negative emotions, helping us recognize and become familiar with their ephemeral nature.

There are two ways to practice cutting through, the second method for gaining familiarity with our inherent nature. First, we investigate our mind. If a thought or emotion is present, we ask ourselves: Where is it coming from? Where is it now? Where is it going? What does it look like? What color is it? When we ask these questions of external objects, we expect to get an answer; but when asked of thoughts and emotions, no answer comes. When that happens, the thought or emotion naturally dissolves without a trace. In this way, we come to recognize that all thoughts and emotions are empty of substance and location. The second way of cutting through is more direct. Rather than asking questions about a thought, we look directly at it. In the moment that we look, it instantly dissolves. This is the technique of looking directly at thought (purjom) that we discussed in chapter 6.

The third way to familiarize ourselves with our inherent nature is called "self-liberating." As taught by my grandfather, this technique is simply to accept a thought as it arises. This means that we neither grasp the thought nor try to push it away. We simply let it be as it is. If we are successful, the thought simply disappears. Applying this method repeatedly, we discover that all things arising in our mind—including thoughts, disturbing emotions, sadness, and misery—are mere appearances. They come. They leave. Just relax and let them come and go. Don't try to investigate. Don't look at them deliberately. Just be calm and relaxed, and let go. In this way, thoughts and emotions self-liberate.

We need not practice these three methods for becoming familiar with our inherent nature in a linear, progressive way. They are like tools we can pull out of our toolbox to deal with situations as needed. Beginning meditators often experience disturbing emotions as their greatest obstacle. In these situations, it is good to use the first method of applying the specific antidote to the specific emotion. But as we gain more experience, we can use each of the three methods as needed. When we do, it isn't necessary to see negative emotions in a negative light. For example, when anger arises, rather than reacting to it negatively—and thereby creating additional negative emotion—simply be aware, noting, "Oh, anger is here." Then, when you investigate the thought accompanying the anger, that thought will simply disappear. You will see that anger is born of the mind. It might linger for a while, but then it will completely dissipate. If we don't follow it and fixate on it, it doesn't have the power to overwhelm us or influence our lives.

These methods share the goals of improving our character, transforming our mind, and recognizing the mind's nature. Applying antidotes counteracts our negative emotions and reduces the tendency of ego-clinging. Looking directly at emotions and thoughts in the moment they arise enables us to see their empty nature. Further investigating the mind by examining the location, color, and shape of negative thoughts and emotions allows them to dissipate before they have a chance to fully emerge.

Recognizing a thought's empty nature is the entryway to carefree ease. When a thought dissolves, it is like watching an isolated drop of water return to the ocean. The infinite and vast ocean, like our unborn wisdom, remains unchanging. We recognize that thoughts and emotions are fleeting appearances arising from a myriad of causes and conditions. They have no substantial existence; they are empty by nature.

By the time we have mastered our mind using these three techniques—applying antidotes, cutting through, and self-liberating—carefree ease arises in full. At this point, our mind's natural clarity is fully illuminated. We can instinctively distinguish between dignity and pride, noticing and judging, selfish happiness and compassionate happiness. Our meditation practice and day-to-day activities are in balance. With carefree ease, our dignity arises effortlessly.

Great Master Attitude

Fear hinders meditation. This is no surprise. I have learned that many people are afraid—of life, religion, death, bureaucracy, themselves, even their meditative experiences. I think that fear manifests when people don't trust themselves. Their dignity is not yet stable. They think their nature is impure. In these situations, the only solution is to remind a person again and again: "Your nature is pure."

It is obvious that fear hinders meditation, but you might be surprised that hope does too. Hope and fear are interdependent, like two sides of one coin. Hoping for a result generates the fear that it won't come about. If our hope has no attachment, then it can be helpful for improving our practice. But be careful—it is very easy to attach to hope, sometimes very subtly. To be free of attachment to fear and hope, we need to develop what I call the "great master attitude."

The great master attitude is to approach meditation with an open mind and heart, without attaching to or evaluating our experience. When meditation is going well and we experience calmness or clarity, we should remind ourselves that this is merely an experience. Don't become excited. Experiences are fleeting. When meditation is not going well—for example, we cannot concentrate and are constantly distracted—we should apply the same attitude and remind ourselves that this is merely an experience. Don't become depressed. Experiences are fleeting.

All sorts of experiences arise in meditation—some pleasant, some unpleasant. Often, nothing happens at all. Detaching from pleasant, unpleasant, or neutral experiences frees us from expectation and judgment. With the great master attitude, we continue to apply the instruction and train repeatedly, but without expecting any result. "Is my meditation working?" This is a question many students have asked. Paradoxically, not expecting a result is the best way to experience real transformation. Real transformation takes time; it is a long-term endeavor. Hoping that something happens only creates a burden on our meditation practice. Thinking too much fuels fear. Then we find ourselves caught in a cycle of hope and fear, the ground of which is our unstable dignity.

The great master attitude is a practical, realistic approach to meditation. Tensing up and sitting like an immovable stone would be pointless. Relax. Bring awareness to whatever your mind is doing or feeling. If your feet are numb from sitting cross-legged, be aware of it; if irritation arises as a result, notice that too. You can move your legs to free them from numbness, but do it mindfully. If you get distracted, refocus, and bring your attention back to your meditation. Just come back. This is the key. What matters is to train again and again, without attachment to hope or fear. Then one day you will begin to see improvements in your attitude and behavior. Your mind will become flexible and adaptable to whatever arises in life, no matter how dramatic.

Many people treat meditation as a project, another goal to achieve. But this goal-oriented attitude defeats the purpose of meditation. We should always remember: *The purpose of meditation is to master our mind, not a technique.* If our goal is to master a technique, we will always be checking our experience to see how we're doing. But to master our mind, we let go of all expectation, dropping all attachment to our experience. This is the great master attitude.

Writing on Water

My grandfather Tulku Urgyen Rinpoche was known for his openness and warmth. He welcomed whoever came to visit him, without exception, even when he himself was critically ill. On one occasion, my grandfather was with a student when an old Tibetan woman came to visit. Walking with a cane, she had gray hair and a deeply wrinkled face. A few moments later, another Tibetan woman arrived. She was young and beautiful.

The student asked my grandfather, "Rinpoche, do you see the old woman and the young lady as different?"

My grandfather replied, "Yes, I certainly see the difference. But in my mind, it's like trying to write my name on the surface of water. If you try to write your name on water, it just disappears, without any trace."

We sometimes think that we should block our thoughts and emotions so that they don't trouble our mind. Actually, it is guaranteed that thoughts and emotions will come no matter how much effort we exert to block them. So we let them come, let them be, and let them go. In this way, thoughts and emotions liberate themselves, like writing on water.

Don't think that when thoughts and emotions come, they will announce their departure so that you can have a good look at the nature of mind. We must learn to free every thought and emotion in the moment it arises, using them as blessed opportunities to see the source of our troubled mind and free ourselves from it. This way, the self-imposed limitation of who we think we are fades away, and we experience more openness and greater clarity from the inside.

DIGNITY TRAINING

Drop. Be. Rest.

As mentioned earlier, there are two ways of cultivating dignity—one with effort, and one without effort. We can cultivate dignity without effort by simply learning how to rest. In Buddhism, resting means staying in our pure state, the state of genuine joy and peace.

> Sit in a comfortable position. Look into space, and rest in that space.
> Relax your eyes, other parts of your body, and your mind. Let your mind rest without doing anything or trying to change anything. Relax and breathe naturally.
> When thoughts come, drop them. When emotions such as anxiety, fear, or discomfort arise, drop them. Don't think about the past, the future, or the present moment. Let go of all sense of time. Simply drop everything, even the idea of meditation.

> The moment you are free of all thought activity (including thinking that you are meditating), in a split second you will experience complete spaciousness. If you don't recognize anything, it is not a problem. If you do recognize something in that moment, such as clarity, drop that too.

> Don't be upset if you are distracted. Simply do not follow the distraction. Whatever arises, there is no need to follow or reject. Just drop it, and let it be.

Gradually, you will see that everything you experience is mind. Completely dropping all mental activity results in the experience of vivid clarity, freshness, and spaciousness. This is the mind's nature. In the mind's nature, there is nothing to hold on to, nothing to look for. Without forcing anything, without fabricating anything, everything is as it is. *Drop. Be. Rest.* Do this repeatedly, without any expectation. You will begin to see that whatever obstructs your mind can never obstruct the mind's wisdom nature. Seeing this vividly enables you to truly rest in the pure state of wisdom and dignity, the true home to who and what you really are.

Bliss Meditation

When your dignity is steady, negative emotions abandoned, and mind at rest in its natural state, a feeling of bliss can briefly arise—mysteriously and spontaneously. The signs of bliss are a tranquil heart, a feeling of utter joy and contentment, and immense happiness. Your heart feels complete satisfaction, as if you have achieved everything you need to achieve in this life, with nothing left undone. Although we may experience bliss as fleeting, the reality is that our nature is flawless bliss. We simply don't see it most of the time.

Generally, a person who has bliss is necessarily happy, but a happy person does not necessarily have bliss. You don't have to hope bliss will happen by itself. Bliss can be cultivated in both our body and our mind through bliss meditation. The practice itself is very simple:

> First, sit in a comfortable position. Breathe naturally to calm your body and mind.
> Turn your mind inward and recall all the richness in your life.
> Next, visualize a cup at the crown of your head filled with warm and blissful oil. Imagine the oil coming down slowly in a straight line from the top of your head to your heart. Traditionally, the channel from the head to the heart is called the central channel.
> As the oil enters the heart center and warms the heart, it creates a pleasant, blissful sensation, like a healing nectar.
> Continue this practice for five to ten minutes.

This bliss meditation can be done at any time of day. It is especially helpful for overcoming anxiety, fear, loneliness, or grumpiness. It helps to transform poisonous thoughts and emotions into medicine through its purifying effect. The result is a feeling of total openness, lightness, and oneness with the world—a profound feeling that life is rich, beautiful, and meaningful.

Inspirational Support

Calm and self-control are signs of listening to the Dharma;
Few passions, signs of meditation;
Harmony with everyone is the sign of a practitioner;
Your mind at ease, the sign of accomplishment.

DUDJOM RINPOCHE[2]

14

Continuing the Journey Home

Each instant, put your heart into it again.
Each moment, remind yourself again.
Each second, check yourself again.
Night and day, make your resolve again.
In the morning, commit yourself again.
Each meditation session, examine mind minutely.
Never be apart from dharma, not even accidentally.
Continually, do not forget.

PATRUL RINPOCHE[1]

If you have read this far, there is a good chance you are interested in continuing your journey home. Of course, this is not the "home" of our conventional understanding—the residence where we grew up, or our current apartment or house. This home is our true nature, the place we've always been but haven't really known until now. We started our search by going outside ourselves, only to realize we need to look inward. This 180-degree turn positions us to discover that the place we seek has been here all along.

By now, hopefully you see how valuable a refuge your dignity is. It is the true home to which you can always return, regardless of whatever circumstances may arise in your life. You may receive a promotion or a demotion. You may be happy or sad, struggling or at peace. When you are at home in your dignity—staying grounded in your good heart, in your mind's true nature—you can notice whatever is happening and respond appropriately.

By studying, contemplating, and engaging the dignity training exercises in the previous chapters, you may have gained some understanding of what dignity is. It's possible you have experienced it directly. If so, the ways you perceive yourself and the world around you may have started to shift, even as everything looks the same on the surface. Regardless of what you have experienced to this point, continuing the journey home requires a sincere willingness to open and soften your heart. For this process, you need courage and discipline, combined with a particular kind of inner strength and curiosity. These qualities arise from your dignity, so embracing them already orients you to home.

Before continuing the journey to fully realizing dignity, it is important to recognize that intellectual knowledge alone will not improve your experience. No matter what you hear or read, including the material in this book, unless you put what you learn into practice, the benefit will be limited. It is essential that you meditate. This is the way to gain direct experience. This direct experience will then deepen your capacity to understand and assimilate what you learn, which in turn will deepen your meditation practice further. This is how you progress.

Three Levels of Meditative Experience

When meditating, it is common to go through three levels of experience. At the first level, when you are a beginner, you may be so accustomed to dwelling in distraction that you fail to recognize being distracted. Is it good news when a beginner thinks their mind is calm? Not really. In this instance, it simply means the mind is too dull to see the comings and goings of thoughts and emotions. You have not yet brought awareness to mind. You do not see the workings of your mind, let alone mind's nature. You are too caught up in the habit of not seeing. That's okay. Meditation will correct this.

After meditating regularly for some time, you come to the second level of meditation experience. Now you have started to see thoughts and emotions. In fact, you may be overwhelmed by how many there are! Is that good or bad? I'd say this is good. You have started gaining awareness of what is really going on in your mind. When this happens, your senses become sharper. You notice more vividly how busy your mind is. Some of this activity can be unpleasant, but you shouldn't be discouraged. This is a sign that your meditation is working. Therefore, at the second level of experience, you can see that your mind is chaotic, but you still can't see your mind's genuine nature.

More time passes. Finally, you reach the third level of meditation experience. Although thoughts still arise in meditation, they no longer create obstacles or cause distraction. You have learned how to stay relaxed, letting thoughts come and go, resulting in a mind that is calm and clear. You may even experience periods of having no thoughts at all and having glimpses of your nature. As you continue practicing, you can stay in the state of carefree ease for longer and longer periods of time. This is very good news. Now you are experiencing the fruit of meditation. This third level of experience allows you to see both your mind and your mind's nature.

Some people are distraught by not seeing progress in their meditation practice. But they may simply have a misguided notion of what progress looks like. The paradox is that not seeing progress can be a sign of progress. In fact, progress may even look opposite to what you would expect. For example, after starting to meditate, you may begin seeing inner conflicts arising from old habitual patterns. When you get a clear view of these, you might think that your meditation is not working. But it really means that you are now able and willing to clearly see what is happening in your moment-to-moment experience. You are recognizing aspects of yourself or your experience that you had previously ignored or suppressed. This is progress. Progress is not always about action. Progress can be gauged by your capacity to "just be." Nothing to do. Nothing to improve. Let be. As it is.

"As it is" does not mean "anything goes." For example, it's not a license to become angry and feel good about that. "As it is" means knowing how to be in a state of nonaction. We usually act from habit, or in a way that reinforces habit. By learning to let go and just be, to let be "as it is," all habitual action is transcended. Then we are in our natural state. This is the ultimate purpose of Buddhist meditation and the purpose of dignity training and practice.

Diligence in Daily Training and Practice

A student once asked me, "How can I achieve the fruit of meditation in a short period of time." I said, "Give fully." By giving fully, I mean exerting oneself fully in dignity training and practice, according to one's individual capacities. During individual training sessions, we should be completely present, giving meditation our full attention; over time, we should diligently train every day. This is how we continually build on our progress. If we want to be an excellent athlete, we must diligently train our body. If we want to be an accomplished musician, we must regularly practice our instrument. If we want to gain dignity quickly, it is crucial that we commit to regular, sustained training and practice.

Keep in mind that, as I defined them earlier, "training" refers to formal meditation while "practice" is what you do at all other times when you're not training. Your aspiration should be to practice all the time, applying what you have gained through formal training in your day-to-day life, liberating yourself from whatever difficulties arise. When you commit yourself in this way, it is easy to gauge how well your formal training is progressing. There is no benefit in meditating if it doesn't change you in positive ways. Seeing positive changes in your conduct and mental attitude is a definite sign of progress. These changes reflect the cultivation of your inner dignity.

What is going to drive these changes? Diligence. You must train every day, day in and day out, no matter what. We all need consistency, commitment, and perseverance to achieve anything in life, and meditation training is no exception. Otherwise, it is easy to stray back into ordinary confusion. When this happens, all progress is lost, and we must start over again. We often waver in our commitments, which creates doubt and hesitation. But when we are fully committed to meditating every day, that brings a tremendous sense of freedom. Train when you are happy; train when you are unhappy. It doesn't matter. You simply train. This is diligence.

Discipline in Daily Training and Practice

In addition to diligence, you must have discipline when engaging in dignity training and practice. Diligence and discipline may seem similar, but there is an important distinction. Whereas diligence applies to how fully we devote ourselves, discipline applies to how well we conduct ourselves—the essence of discipline is accepting responsibility for everything we do, whether we are talking, acting, or thinking. Accepting this responsibility requires that we constantly check our mind, noticing our habits and taking care of our emotions. Our habits and emotions color our experience and impact how we perceive ourselves, others, and the world. Realize that the distortions created by our habits and emotions also arise during our meditation sessions. For example, if we are angry, our meditation is angry. Therefore, we must check all aspects of our conduct—our thinking, our speech, our actions, our way of being—both on and off the cushion.

The Buddha taught discipline by dividing it into three categories: (1) do no harm, (2) do good, and (3) tame your mind. The first category, do no harm, essentially means to be a decent human being. Don't do anything that might be hurtful or damaging to another person. I have seen people become so wrapped up in spirituality and meditation practice that they forget about those who are important to them. I don't think this can be justified. It's important to balance spiritual practice with your significant relationships, including family and friends. And do your best not to harm anyone in any way.

The second category of discipline is to do good. Going beyond merely not causing harm, we strive to benefit others to the best of our ability. We cherish goodness and strive to cultivate generosity, compassion, and other positive qualities in our meditation practice. Then we bring these qualities to bear in helping others, according to our best ability and what would be skillful in the given situation.

The third category of discipline, to tame (or transform) your mind, is the main purpose of dignity training. If you improve your training but don't transform your mind, the training has gone wrong. The duration of your meditation session is less important than how genuinely and sincerely you train and how effective your training is. Remember that the goal of meditation is to master your mind, not to master the technique. There is no point in becoming a "good" meditator if you don't become kinder, gentler, and more compassionate.

Scheduling Your Day

Structuring your day is important for making effective progress with your dignity training and practice. Here are some suggestions.

When you wake up each morning, check your motivation and set your day's intention. How are you going to use the next twenty-four hours to make this day meaningful? How can you ensure this day is used well and not wasted? Setting your intention at the beginning of each day reaffirms your commitment to practice.

During the day, it is vital that you conduct your dignity training at a regular time. Designate the duration of your session in advance—ten minutes, twenty minutes, one hour, or whatever amount of time works for you. Your training session is an opportunity to give full attention to being with yourself, so be sure to arrange your time and space accordingly.

In addition, it is important to check your conduct throughout the day. Are you putting what you know into practice? What is your reaction to making mistakes? Perhaps you say: "I am such a bad person!" It will be hard to make progress with this attitude. Better would be something like: "Oh, well, I made a few mistakes, but I can change because I have dignity." If you respond to mistakes in this way, you will begin to really see yourself, like yourself, and fully accept yourself. Fully accepting yourself doesn't mean accepting your bad habits and confusion because these are not you. It means accepting and embracing your genuine self, the dignified you.

At the end of the day, before going to bed, review the day's activities. If you find that you have made mistakes, apply the four powers as explained in chapter 11 to generate remorse and resolve not to make the same mistakes again. If you have done good deeds, rejoice and dedicate the merit of these good deeds to the benefit of all beings. It is important to go to bed without regrets or agitation. Remind yourself that you are dignity, and you have never been separated from it. Go to sleep with confidence and certainty in the dignity in your heart.

Both training and practice require that we shift our focus from thinking about our ordinary worries and difficulties to understanding the mind and its nature. Doing so on a daily basis enhances our experience of dignity. The key is maintaining steady, consistent effort without grasping at the result. The goal is to neither be dejected by poor practice nor elated by strong practice.

Then we become our own master and not the victim of others' opinions or our own fleeting emotions. At that point, the effect of our meditation will show in our daily life. We will be more content and at ease, and our qualities of compassion and love will shine naturally. This is the sign that we are improving and that our meditation experience, behavior, and view are in harmony.

The Benefits of Retreat

Many of us are constantly busy with activities. Contemporary cultures often praise productivity, and, as a result, work tends to invade all aspects of our lives. When we are not working, our busy ways of entertaining ourselves can feel like another form of work. This is expressed in the popular expression "Work hard, play hard." Try to remember that we are here to live, not achieve goals. Of course, we must make a living, but we must also be careful not to substitute making a living for simply living. If we apply the conventional mindset to our meditation training, it will be easy to see the pursuit of dignity as just another project, job, or goal to achieve. Of course, this is not the case. A very beneficial practice to counteract these tendencies is to retreat from our usual, mundane activities.

The point of retreat is to have uninterrupted time to be alone and to reconnect with our true nature in a safe and secluded place. This kind of retreat is unfamiliar to many people. A student told me of a time she was happily doing a personal retreat in a Catholic monastery. Another retreat participant showed up, but she was not as happy. She was baffled by the bleak, simple setup of the monastery: no swimming pool, no spa, no gourmet meals. This wasn't at all what she had expected. She didn't know what to do with herself. Within a day, she left.

It's unfortunate that this person never got to experience the magic of retreat. In retreat, we have the rare opportunity to give undivided attention to ourselves—to listen deeply to our inner thoughts, clearly see our habitual patterns, and reconnect with our true nature. Having time for contemplation in a silent setting without external distraction is precious nowadays. Looking inward to know ourselves is an optimal way to cultivate dignity; paradoxically, it also deepens our understanding of the outer world and of other people in it.

It isn't necessary for a retreat to involve complete isolation from other people. Another option is to engage in group retreat. This form of retreat offers the same opportunity to step back from our usual activities and be with our deepest self, the true home of our dignity. Whichever form we pursue, retreat enables us to not take thinking so seriously, which results in not taking ourselves so seriously. There's a saying that we tend to see things not as they are but as we are. In retreat, we learn to see things as they are, not as we ordinarily are conditioned to see them.

No matter how much you train and practice, most important is the quality of your experience, not where you train or for how long. Therefore, don't be too concerned if retreat is not possible for you at this time. During your daily training and practice, do a little bit at a time. You'll improve slowly, and this is okay. Many of us have jobs, families to take care of, and bills to pay. It is important to keep a balance between individual spiritual practice and family responsibilities. At the beginning, it is preferable to simply engage in dignity training and practice every day, taking it slowly and gradually. Remember that even small changes in the mind can bring big changes in life. Once your meditation is more stable, you can consider doing a short group retreat, then a longer group retreat. Eventually, you may want to try a personal retreat.

Regardless of whether you are engaging in daily practice or long-term retreat, the key is having more solitude, more time to look inward. This gives rise to a deep desire to integrate dignity into every situation in life. Remember, you can only understand dignity when you experience it. Dignity is your nature; you already have it. When you can rest your mind, dignity is within reach. And it has always been within reach, even though you have been on a journey to find it. According to the Buddhist teaching, there's only one way to reach it—by going inside. Time is very precious. Don't wait until it is too late to know yourself, to know your pure nature, to realize your inherent dignity.

Setting Your Own Course

Almost everyone I know is interested in dignity but for different reasons. What is your interest? Are you simply curious? Do you seek intellectual knowledge? Do you want to know how to assert and protect your human rights? One student told me she wanted to learn about dignity because she is tired of being afraid. Is she interested in a temporary release from fear or an ultimate solution?

You need to know the questions in your heart before you can determine your life's direction and meaning. Before that, external things seem very important. Afterward, when you have gained clear direction in life, external things become less interesting. They lose their power to overwhelm or distract you from your inner qualities. As a rule, when we are clear about the purpose of our existence, we don't feel hollow in our heart.

In Buddhism, the purpose of our existence, and the reason for attaining dignity, is to become fully enlightened. When you are enlightened, you have ultimate dignity; likewise, achieving ultimate dignity is the same as achieving enlightenment. At that point, you have fully conquered your negative emotions and removed all confusion about your own nature and the nature of phenomena. Your love, compassion, wisdom, and dignity are complete. This level of realization generally requires tremendous commitment.

Only you can decide how far you want to go on this journey toward dignity. But realize that no matter your goal or purpose, the path you traverse will not be a straight line. We see this in the physical world. When traveling to distant lands, we may have to cross valleys and mountains, and navigate rivers and gorges. The lay of the land may require that we sometimes go up and sometimes go down. The spiritual path is similar. In this instance, we are traversing the terrain of the mind, and there will be many bends and obstacles to negotiate. Although book learning can provide some understanding and knowledge, we must learn to apply that knowledge to our own immediate experience. If you have a teacher, the teachings from your teacher to you will be easy. But the application that goes from you to yourself is difficult.

Three Stages in the Path to Dignity

My grandfather used to say that sentient begins are like gold mixed with impurities. Our nature is pure gold, meaning that we are already enlightened. But we are temporarily covered with dust and dirt. Everyone can become "re-enlightened" and restore the purity of the gold. Of course, for most of us this is a process. As a kind of map, we can identify three stages in the path to restoring our inherent dignity, the purity of our gold.

At the beginning, you may regard you and your dignity as different. This is because you are accustomed to identifying with ego. As a result, your heart is fragile. You can't separate yourself from the wrong actions or mistakes that you commit, so you are terrified to look at yourself in an open and honest way. Any errors you make seem to demonstrate that something is fundamentally wrong with you. This starting position is one of great discomfort and difficulty, the starting point that often motivates the spiritual path.

With practice, your habitual identification with ego starts to loosen. When you start to glimpse the purity of your essential nature, you have entered the second stage. Prior to this point, you've regarded dignity as a positive potential that lies beyond you; but with this first glimpse, you think, "Maybe my dignity and I are not so separate after all!" As you continue having these experiences, you eventually start to recognize that you really are intrinsically dignified, even as you are still emotionally reactive, quick to judge, and sometimes completely raw and vulnerable. This is good progress. But you haven't completely dismantled the ego structure that has trapped you, and the essential purity of your nature remains largely hidden. Sometimes it seems you and your dignity are one, but usually they still feel separate. More training is needed to embrace your nature and extricate yourself from ego's paranoia.

At the third stage, your practice has become stable. You see that you and your dignity are inseparable. You have shifted your identity to the core of your being, your buddha-nature. There is nothing to fear because you are inherently and intrinsically pure and complete. From that stance, it becomes easier to look at the mischievousness of your imperfect and self-centered ego. You know your ego is not you. Your mistakes are not you. Therefore, there is no reason to feel bad about yourself, even as you might feel remorse for any suffering or confusion you've created for yourself or others. You know you can change your behaviors to align with your nature.

In a nutshell, dignity is certainty in who you really are. The Buddhist teachings on dignity show us how to shift our sense of fundamental identity from the narrow confines of a constrictive ego-self to the wide-open expanses of unshackled buddha-nature. In other words, now we fully embrace and identify with the perfect and complete essence at the core of every sentient existence. This includes you, me, and everyone else. Therefore, even though you train to see yourself, and not someone or something else, once you do see yourself, you also understand the world around you. Dignity is the sense of certainty and trust that arises when we recognize the fundamental purity of our nature beyond any sense of personal identity.

I have been blessed to grow up in a family and community of dedicated practitioners who share the life goal of achieving enlightenment, a goal motivated by the sincere wish to lead others to enlightenment as well. Starting with the Buddha, many teachers of the past and present have pointed out the inherent potential that each of us has and how we can actualize it. They see us as pure and complete; their kindness, respect, and patience convince us it is possible to change, improve, and become like them. It is possible to be sincere, relaxed, and aware in every situation in life. It is possible to accept and appreciate who we are. It is possible to be joyful and at peace.

When our intrinsic dignity is fully actualized, we can be at home in the world and truly benefit others. But we must remember that teachers cannot do the job for us. It is up to us to travel the road ourselves and experience what they have experienced. They have done it, and so can we.

The great teachers we have met in the world enable us to see our ultimate teacher—our innate wisdom and dignity. One such outer teacher was Marpa, a great Tibetan Buddhist master and translator of the eleventh century. With no discrimination and with complete equanimity, Marpa made the aspiration that everyone who practices should become better than he himself, meaning that they should surpass his own level of realization. I have always felt inspired by this aspiration, and I've made it my guiding wish in writing this book. With that thought, here is my heartfelt wish for you:

May you fully cultivate dignity, realize your true nature, and become better than I myself.

DIGNITY TRAINING EXERCISES

Part One: **Your Nature Is Pure**

Chapter 1:   Your Relationship with Inner Dignity   22

Chapter 2:   Making Aspiration   41

Chapter 3:   A New Mantra   53

Chapter 4:   Meditation Posture   61

             Gentle Focus Meditation   63

Part Two: **You Can Change**

Chapter 5:   Breathing to Restore Balance
between Body and Mind   83

             Tame an Emotion   84

Chapter 6:   Looking Directly at Thoughts   94

             Looking Directly at Emotions   95

Chapter 7:   Meditation on Loving-Kindness and
Compassion   103

Chapter 8:   Meditation on the Four Immeasurable
Qualities of Love   122

Chapter 9:   Analytic Meditation   139

Chapter 10:   Tonglen: The Art of Giving and Taking   159

Part Three: **Gaining Certainty and Trust**

Chapter 11:   Open Awareness   182

Chapter 12:   Contemplating Death   197

Chapter 13:   Drop. Be. Rest.   208

             Bliss Meditation   209

NOTES

PART ONE: YOUR NATURE IS PURE

1. Lhasey Lotsawa Translations and Publications, trans., *The Noble Wisdom of the Time of Death Sūtra and Commentaries by Prajñā-samudra and Śāntideva* (Kathmandu, Nepal: Lhasey Lotsawa Translations and Publications, 2015), 7.

Chapter 1: The Mirror of the Heart

1. Antoine de Saint Exupéry, *The Little Prince*, trans. Katherine Woods (San Diego: Harcourt Brace Jovanovich, 1971), 87.
2. Ruth Macklin, "Dignity Is a Useless Concept," *British Medical Journal* 327 (December 20, 2003), 1419–20.
3. Martin Luther King Jr., "What Is Your Life's Blueprint?" (speech, Barratt Junior High School, Philadelphia, PA, October 26, 1967), https://projects.seattletimes.com/mlk/words-blueprint.html.
4. Cited in Michael Rosen, *Dignity: Its History and Meaning* (Cambridge, MA: Harvard University Press, 2012), 2.
5. Tulku Urgyen Rinpoche, *Blazing Splendor: The Memoirs of the Dzogchen Yogi Tulku Urgyen Rinpoche,* as told to Erik Pema Kunsang and Marcia Binder Schmidt (Kathmandu: Rangjung Yeshe Publications, 2005), xxi.

Chapter 2: Know Yourself

1. Śāntideva, *Bodhicaryāvatāra: An Introduction to the Bodhisattva's Way of Life*, trans. Adam Pearcey (Lotsawa House, 2007), chap. 3, www.lotsawahouse.org/indian-masters/shantideva/bodhicharyavatara-3.

Chapter 3: Beyond the Beautiful and the Ugly

1. Longchenpa, *Finding Rest in the Nature of the Mind,* trans. Padmakara Translation Group (Boulder, CO: Shambhala, 2017), 206.

2. Thinley Norbu, *White Sail: Crossing the Waves of Ocean Mind to the Serene Continent of the Triple Gems* (Boston: Shambhala, 2001), 78–79.

Chapter 4: Three Meditation Teachers

1. Chökyi Drakpa, "A Torch for the Path to Omniscience," trans. Adam Pearcey (Lotsawa House, 2000: revised 2021), www .lotsawahouse.org/tibetan-masters/chokyi-drakpa/a-torch -for-the-path.
2. Khenchen Palden Sherab Rinpoche and Khenpo Tsewang Dongyal Rinpoche, *The Buddhist Path: A Practical Guide from the Nyingma Tradition of Tibetan Buddhism*, ed. Ann Helm and Michael White (Ithaca, NY: Snow Lion, 2010), 28.

PART TWO: YOU CAN CHANGE

1. Gampopa, *The Jewel Ornament of Liberation*, ed. Ani K. Trinlay Chödron, trans. Khenpo Konchog Gyaltsen Rinpoche (Boston: Snow Lion, 1998), 159.

Chapter 5: Making Friends with "Sticky Mind"

1. Chögyam Trungpa, *The Myth of Freedom and the Way of Meditation* (Boston: Shambhala, 1988), 104.
2. David Edmonds, "The Science of Addiction: Do You Always Like the Things You Want?" *BBC*, December 12, 2020, www.bbc .com/news/stories-55221825.
3. Dudjom Rinpoche, "A Prayer to Recognize My Own Faults and Keep in Mind the Objects of Refuge," trans. Bhakha Tulku and Constance Wilkinson (Lotsawa House, 1989), www.lotsawahouse.org /tibetan-masters/dudjom-rinpoche/prayer-to-recognize-own-faults.

Chapter 6: Noticing, Not Judging

1. Thich Nhat Hanh, *Being Peace* (Berkeley, CA: Parallax Press, 2005), 69.
2. Thomas Byrom, trans., "Dhammapada," in *Teachings of the Buddha*, ed. Jack Kornfield (Boston: Shambhala, 1996), 4.

Chapter 7: Healing from the Habit of Judgment

1. The Dzogchen Ponlop Rinpoche, "Entering the Trainings in Compassion," in Jamgon Kongtrul et al., *Trainings in Compassion:*

Manuals on the Meditation of Avalokiteshvara, trans. Tyler Dewar (Ithaca, NY: Snow Lion, 2004), 21.

Chapter 8: The Courage to Love

1. His Holiness the Dalai Lama, *In My Own Words: An Introduction to My Teachings and Philosophy*, ed. Rajiv Mehrotra (Carlsbad, CA: Hay House, 2008), 15.
2. Dzigar Kongtrul Rinpoche, *Uncommon Happiness* (Kathmandu: Rangjung Yeshe Publications, 2009), 94.

Chapter 9: "Who Am I?"

1. Chandrakirti, *Introduction to the Middle Way: Chandrakirti's "Madhyamakavatara" with Commentary by Jamgön Mipham*, trans. Padmakara Translation Group (Boston: Shambhala, 2002), 59.
2. Nicholas Wade, "Your Body Is Younger Than You Think," *New York Times*, August 2, 2005, www.nytimes.com/2005/08/02/science/your-body-is-younger-than-you-think.html.
3. Elizabeth Bernstein, "A Tiny Pronoun Says a Lot about You," *Wall Street Journal*, October 7, 2013, www.wsj.com/articles/SB10001424052702304626104579121371885556170.
4. Khenpo Tsultrim Gyamtso Rinpoche, *Progressive Stages of Meditation on Emptiness*, trans. Shenpen Hookham (Auckland, New Zealand: Zhyisil Chokyi Ghatsal Publications, 2001), 11.

Chapter 10: The Compassion to Act

1. Quoted in Matthieu Ricard, *Altruism: The Power of Compassion to Change Yourself and the World*, trans. Charlotte Mandell and Sam Gordon (New York: Little, Brown, 2013), xi.
2. Chökyi Nyima Rinpoche and David R. Shlim, *Medicine and Compassion*, 2nd ed. (Boston: Wisdom Publications, 2015).
3. Beth A. Lown, Julie Rosen, and John Marttila, "An Agenda for Improving Compassionate Care: A Survey Shows about Half of Patients Say Such Care Is Missing," *Health Affairs* 30, no. 9 (September 2011): 1772–78.
4. Daniel Goleman and Richard J. Davidson, *Altered Traits* (New York: Avery, 2017).

5. Sharon Begley, *Train Your Mind, Change Your Brain* (New York: Ballantine Books, 2007), 212–42.

6. Marianne Spoon, "Training Your Compassion 'Muscle' May Boost Brain's Resilience to Others' Suffering," University of Wisconsin–Madison News, May 22, 2018, https://centerhealthyminds.org /news/training-your-compassion-muscle-may-boost-brains -resilience-in-the-face-of-suffering.

7. Thich Nhat Hanh, *Being Peace*, 81.

8. Sue-Sue Tâm Bảo Đàn, *The Lama of Many Lifetimes: Touching the Living Heart of Garchen Rinpoche. Book Two: Perfection of Liberation (1958–1980)* (Irvine, CA: Milam Bardo Publications, 2019), 228.

9. Sue-Sue Tâm Bảo Đàn, *Lama of Many Lifetimes*, 228.

10. Shantideva, *The Way of the Bodhisattva: A Translation of the Bodhicharyavatara*, trans. Padmakara Translation Group (Boston: Shambhala, 1997), 128.

PART THREE: GAINING CERTAINTY AND TRUST

1. Khenchen Thrangu, *Luminous Clarity* (Boulder, CO: Snow Lion, 2016), 79.

Chapter 11: Authentic Power

1. Toni Morrison, "The Truest Eye," interview by Pam Houston, *O. The Oprah Magazine*, November 2003, p. 4, www.oprah.com /omagazine/toni-morrison-talks-love/4.

2. The Third Dzogchen Rinpoche, *Great Perfection*, vol. 2, *Separation and Breakthrough*, trans. Cortland Dahl (Ithaca, NY: Snow Lion, 2008), 180.

Chapter 12: Dignified Living and Dying

1. Sushila Blackman, ed., *Graceful Exits: How Great Beings Die* (New York: Weatherhill, 1997), 62.

2. For Martin's blog, see http://martinsidwell.com.

3. *The Noble Wisdom of the Time of Death Sūtra and Commentaries by Prajñāsamudra and Śāntideva*, 3–7.

4. *The Noble Wisdom of the Time of Death Sūtra and Commentaries by Prajñāsamudra and Śāntideva*, 5.

5. *The Noble Wisdom of the Time of Death Sūtra and Commentaries by Prajñāsamudra and Śāntideva*, 5.

6. *The Noble Wisdom of the Time of Death Sūtra and Commentaries by Prajñāsamudra and Śāntideva*, 5-7.

7. *The Noble Wisdom of the Time of Death Sūtra and Commentaries by Prajñāsamudra and Śāntideva*, 7.

8. *The Noble Wisdom of the Time of Death Sūtra and Commentaries by Prajñāsamudra and Śāntideva*, 7.

9. Dilgo Khyentse Rinpoche, *The Heart Treasure of the Enlightened Ones: The Practice of View, Meditation, and Action* (Boston: Shambhala, 1993), 157.

Chapter 13: Carefree Ease

1. Chokgyur Lingpa, "Advice in Brief," in *The Essential Amrita of Profound Meaning: Oral Instructions and Practical Advice Bestowed upon Fortunate Followers, Eye-Opener to What Is to Be Adopted and Abandoned*. https://www.lhaseylotsawa.org/library/advice-in-brief-eng.

2. Dudjom Rinpoche, *Wisdom Nectar: Dudjom Rinpoché's Heart Advice*, trans. Ron Garry (Boulder, CO: Snow Lion, 2005), 80.

Chapter 14: Continuing the Journey Home

1. Matthieu Ricard, *Enlightened Vagabond: The Life and Teachings of Patrul Rinpoche* (Boulder, CO: Shambhala, 2017), 151.

ABOUT THE AUTHORS

PHAKCHOK RINPOCHE is a popular and beloved spiritual teacher with a style that is at once unique, dynamic, and engaging. Born in 1981 in Kathmandu, Nepal, Rinpoche was recognized soon after birth—at the early age of one—as the seventh Phakchok Rinpoche, the reincarnation of a great meditation master. He completed traditional Tibetan Buddhist education at age twenty-three and since then has taught Buddhist philosophy, theory, and practice in centers and universities worldwide. He also directs several monasteries and practice centers in Asia, North America, and South America. Rinpoche's sharp insight into contemporary global culture makes his teachings unusually accessible and relatable to our everyday lives and concerns. He works diligently to preserve Buddhist scholarship through the administration of Lhasey Lotsawa Translations and Publications (cofounded with his father, Tsikey Chokling Rinpoche) and oversees humanitarian projects that include running a free health clinic, offering education to monastics, and providing emergency relief for victims of natural disasters.

Trained in Chinese intellectual history at the University of Wisconsin-Madison, SOPHIE (SHU-CHIN) WU, PHD, teaches Asian history and philosophy, including Buddhism, as an associate professor at Agnes Scott College. Her current academic research focuses on Chinese and Tibetan independent films and contemplative education. As a longtime student of Buddhism, Sophie is a board member and meditation instructor for Phakchok Rinpoche's organization. She lives in Atlanta with her husband. In her (imaginary) free time, Sophie enjoys home-roasted coffee, nature hikes, and traveling.

For more information about Awakening Dignity events and activities, please visit www.awakeningdignity.org.